THE BEST
WNES
IN THE
SUPER
MARKETS
2010

THE BEST WINES IN THE SUPER MARKETS 2010

NED HALLEY

foulsham
LONDON • NEW YORK • TORONTO • SYDNEY

foulsham

The Oriel, Thames Valley Court,
183–187 Bath Road, Slough SL1 4AA

Foulsham books can be found in all good bookshops and
direct from www.foulsham.com

ISBN: 978-0-572-03535-8

Text copyright © 2010 Ned Halley

Series, format and layout design
copyright © 2010 W. Foulsham & Co. Ltd

Printed by Printwise (Haverhill) Limited, Haverhill

Contents

What we want is wine
── we can afford ──

The wine tastings generously staged each year by the supermarket chains are an invaluable source for writers like me. In the space of a few weeks, I get to try a substantial proportion of all the new wines or new vintages appearing on the shelves, including the freshly bottled wines from the European harvests of the previous autumn.

Also at the tastings I can chat to the clever young people who work in the supermarkets' wine departments. With science degrees or MBAs (or both) and honours including the exacting Master of Wine qualification, they are the wine trade's front line, experts in production (all major supermarkets now send their own consultants into their suppliers' wineries) and in marketing, perpetually adjusting their ranges to the shifting tastes of a fickle public.

This year, there has been a distinct theme to the talk about the market. It is, naturally enough, value for money. Wine is getting more expensive, thanks to punitive duty (£1.61 a bottle since the 2009 Budget, the highest in the developed world) and a bad run for sterling against the euro and the US dollar. And this is not a good time for supermarkets to impose price rises. Worldwide economic downturn, burgeoning UK unemployment and chronic indebtedness are conspiring to halt the gentle rise in wine consumption that over a generation has transformed us, just about, into a wine-drinking nation.

In 2008, Britain became the world's biggest importer of wine, overtaking Germany by shipping in 1.6 billion bottles. We are now accustomed to wine, even though we consume less than half as much, per capita, as the French, Italians or

Spanish do. But then we are not, like them, living in a wine-producing country. Yes, it's true that English and Welsh vineyards have expanded in area by 50 per cent in the last five years, to nearly 3,000 acres. And some of our home-grown sparkling wines are jolly good. The less said about our still wines, the better. But we will never be a wine-producing nation on a significant scale – even the most optimistic forecasts, of five million bottles a year by 2015, represent less than a third of one per cent of current consumption.

And even our estimable achievement in becoming the world's leading importer might not endure for long. A 2009 survey for the Wine & Spirit Trade Association reveals that a third of wine consumers are admitting to spending less on wine. And the trend is not benefiting demand for cheaper wines. Sales of bottles costing under £4 fell 11 per cent between 2008 and 2009. The Association's chief executive, Jeremy Beadles, gloomily concludes that 'many people on lower budgets are simply being forced out of the wine category'.

Individual managers among the supermarkets are cagey about their trading figures. They don't like to admit to losing market share, especially to their nearest rivals. But what they do all admit is that demand has sunk faster than any of them can remember. They acknowledge, however, that it could be worse. Because higher taxes and draconian new regulations are strangling the pub and restaurant trades, damage to supermarket wine sales is unquestionably being limited by the choice millions of consumers are making to drink at home rather than going out.

Maybe it is this marginal mercy to the retailers that is enabling them to stay in the game. Prices on the shelf really have not greatly increased. Somebody is absorbing the costs of the hikes in duty and the swings in the sterling exchange rate. Politely enquiring of the teams at the tastings, I get the universal impression that it is not the supermarkets making sacrifices; it's the producers. For many of them, UK retail multiples are their most important customers. If the buyer says all he or she can pay for this year's vintage is X, due to circumstances beyond our control, you understand, what can the producer say?

There is a school of thought that if you pay winemakers peanuts, you'll get the wine you deserve. In this case, it should mean that the new vintages I have been tasting in 2009 would be noticeably inferior to their predecessors. Well, they aren't. If anything, quality and variety simply seem to improve year on year. There are far fewer faulty or merely boring wines than I remember from the bad old days.

Standards are high, prices are keen, and the discounts that have done so much to drive demand for wine in the good years are as persistent as ever. Sure, there are plenty of offers of wines artificially inflated in price and then halved back to their original value – I do wish respectable retailers wouldn't insult the intelligence of their customers by doing this – but there are genuine promotions, too, on proper wines quite clearly being sold at very low margins indeed.

And there are new wines tailored to current market conditions. I have liked Sainsbury's very cheap French 1.5-litre ribbed-plastic bottles, a real throwback to the 1960s except for the impressive quality, and Waitrose have launched new wines from Chile and California under the label 'Virtue': they are shipped in tank to Britain and bottled in lightweight glass, minimising carbon footprint as well as cost. Asda's new 'Smart Price' wines cost under £3, and are perfectly respectable, and Tesco launched a 'Value' range of Spanish wines in juice-style cartons at £2.89 back in the autumn.

Some of these wines have made it into this edition of *The Best Wines in the Supermarkets*, and I have, naturally, been especially on the lookout for bargains, picking out Top Tens of wines under £4 as an additional feature this year. But the main business of this book is, as ever, to pick out the best wines principally on the basis of how good they are.

Most of the wines scoring 9 or 10 points are in the price

range of £5 to £10 because to qualify for top scores, every bottle must deliver exceptional value as well as exceptional quality. If a wine above £10 does reach the heights, you can rest assured I considered it very, very good, because even in the best of times I find it a painful wrench to hand over more than a tenner for any wine bought in a supermarket.

To make the book as simple a reference source as possible, I am sticking to the formula of arranging the listings under the names of the retailers, then within each of these entries grouping the wines by colour, then by nation of origin, in ascending price order. This more or less coincides with the way the supermarkets display the wines on their shelves.

More than in any previous edition, the 2010 guide concentrates on own-brand wines. These are, obviously enough, the only ones that are exclusive to the respective retailers, but equally importantly, I am beginning to find that they represent the best value in the supermarkets. They are very often made with direct interference from the retailers' consultant winemakers, and so they reflect the wine departments' philosophies, which is interesting. And the prices are, I suspect, thoroughly screwed down. Wines exclusive to big UK customers are no doubt made to a fixed sterling price; even if, say, the euro rises sharply, continental wine producers must be in an awkward position to argue about more money when both sides know the wines could not be sold anywhere else if the contract were voided.

Anyway, should we worry ourselves about the welfare of foreign winemakers? We are in the grip of a terrible economic, political and social downturn, and deserve an affordable glass of wine in consolation.

As before in introducing each edition, I must apologise in advance for the fact that some of the wines I have recommended will have sold out or been replaced with a more recent vintage by the time you are reading this. And it is very likely that prices will have increased (they never decrease) for many of the wines. At the time of writing, the Government had made no commitment about excise duty on alcohol, which was raised in 2008 to cancel out any reduction in price following the cut in VAT from 17.5 per cent to 15 per cent introduced as a temporary stimulus to the economy. Whether the reversion to 17.5 per cent in January 2010 will be (or has been, depending on when you are reading this) accompanied by a corresponding cut in excise duty, is unclear. My bet, for what it is worth, is that no UK government will ever reduce the duty on alcohol.

And finally, let me add that everything I say in this book about the wines and about the retailers is based on nothing more than my own knowledge and understanding. Taste in all things is personal, and more so in wine than in other respects. But I hope the impressions I have given of the 500-or-so wines recommended in this guide will tempt readers to look beyond the ubiquitous brands that populate far too much space on supermarket shelves (and very little space in this book) and to discover some of the genuine, individual wines that really are worth paying for.

—*It's all about variety*—

This book categorises the wines by nation of origin. This is largely to follow the manner in which retailers arrange their wines, but also because it is the country or region of origin that still most distinguishes one style of wine from another. True, wines are now commonly labelled most prominently with their constituent grape variety, but to classify all the world's wines into the small number of principal grape varieties would make for categories of an unwieldy size.

Chardonnay, Pinot Grigio and Sauvignon Blanc are overwhelmingly dominant among whites, and four grapes – Cabernet Sauvignon, Grenache, Merlot and Syrah (also called Shiraz) – account for a high proportion of red wines made worldwide.

But each area of production still – in spite of creeping globalisation – puts its own mark on its wines. Chardonnays from France remain (for the moment at least) quite distinct from those of Australia. Cabernet Sauvignon grown in a cool climate such as that of Bordeaux is a very different wine from Cabernet cultivated in the cauldron of the Barossa.

Of course there are 'styles' that winemakers worldwide seek to follow. Yellow, oaky Chardonnays of the type pioneered in South Australia are now made in South Africa, too – and in new, high-tech wineries in New Zealand and Chile, Spain and Italy. But the variety is still wide. Even though the 'upfront' high-alcohol wines of the New World have grabbed so much of the market, France continues to make the elegant wines it has always made in its classic regions. Germany still produces racy, delicate Rieslings, and the distinctive zones of Italy, Portugal and Spain make ever more characterful wines from indigenous grapes, as opposed to imported global varieties.

Among less expensive wines, the theme is, admittedly, very much a varietal one. The main selling point for most 'everyday' wines is the grape of origin rather than the country of origin. It makes sense, because the characteristics of various grape varieties do a great deal to identify taste. A bottle of white wine labelled 'Chardonnay' can reasonably be counted on to deliver that distinctive peachy or pineappley smell and soft, unctuous apple flavours. A Sauvignon Blanc should evoke gooseberries, green fruit and grassy freshness. And so on.

For all the domination of Chardonnay and Cabernet, there are plenty of other grape varieties making their presence felt. Argentina, for example, has revived the fortunes of several French and Italian varieties that had become near-extinct at home. And the grape that (in my view) can make the most exciting of white wines, the Riesling, is now doing great things in the southern hemisphere as well as at home in Germany.

Among the current market trends, the rise of rosé continues apace. Now accounting for nearly two out of every ten bottles of still wine sold, the choice of pink brands has simply exploded. I have certainly found a greater number of interesting pinks than might have been imagined a few years ago, but there are still plenty of dull ones with suspiciously high levels of residual sugar.

Rosé wines are supposed to be made from black-skinned grapes. After the crush, the skins are left in contact with the juice for long enough to impart a pleasing colour, and maybe some flavour with it, and the liquids and solids are then separated before the winemaking process continues as it would for white wine.

Some rosés are made merely by blending red and white wines together. Oddly enough, this is how all (bar one or two) pink champagnes are made, as permitted under the local appellation rules. But under prevailing regulations in Europe, the practice is otherwise forbidden. Elsewhere in the world, where winemaking is very much less strictly standardised, blending is no doubt common enough. So common that in 2009 a group of producers lobbied the European Commission to relax the EU-wide ban on blending to make rosé. Their argument was that unregulated producers were competing in the newly booming market with wines of a kind that EU members were in no position to match. The Commission was inclined to agree.

But then came an about-turn. Instead of simply waiving the ban in the interests of commerce, the Commissioner for Agriculture, Mariann Fischer Boel, heeded representations from winemakers in France and Italy. They protested, loudly, that standards should be maintained; the good name of rosé was at stake. In June 2009, Boel made her decision. 'It is important we listen to our producers when they are concerned about changes to regulations,' she announced. 'It has become clear that a majority in our wine sector believe that ending the ban on blending could undermine the image of traditional rosé. I am always prepared to listen to good arguments and that is why I am making this change.'

Never mind the image of rosé, this decision will surely do much to maintain the actual quality of a wine style that needs to conform to high standards. Rosés are doing much to attract new customers to wine overall, and if their introduction is allowed to be via cut-price rubbish made by cheats, the fad for pink wine – the only bright spot in the present market – could soon be extinguished.

It is, I know, a perpetual source of anguish to winemakers in tightly regulated European nations that they have to compete in important markets like Britain with producers in Australia, the Americas and South Africa who can make and label their wines just as they please. Vineyard irrigation, the use of oak chips, the blending in of wines from other continents: all are permitted in the New World and eschewed in the Old.

But would we have it any other way? No winemaker I have met in Bordeaux or Barolo, Bernkastel or Rias Baixas seriously wants to abandon the methods and conventions that make their products unique – even with an eye on creating a global brand. And in this present time of stagnation in the world wine markets, this assurance of enduring diversity is a comfort indeed.

Looking for a —————*favourite wine?*—————

If you have a favourite supermarket wine and hope to find it in this book, check the index starting on page 173.

The index is the most sensible place to start, because many of the wines I have tasted from any given supermarket, and thus entered under that chain's heading, will also be available from one or more of its rivals. I know, for example, that the excellent Spanish white Torres Viña Esmeralda 2008 is sold by Booths at £7.49, but can also be found on the shelves of other retailers. I have listed it under Booths because that's where I tasted it, and to replicate this entry along with many others that are widely stocked, under all the relevant retailers, would crowd the pages with repetitions.

So, if you're interested in a branded wine you remember seeing in, say, Morrisons, don't look only in the very brief entry for that company. Check the index for the wine, and it might just be listed under another retailer's section.

—It's all in the grape—

The character of most wines is defined largely by the grape variety, and it is a source of innocent pleasure to be able to identify which variety it is without peeking at the label. Here are some of the characteristics to look for in wines from the most widely planted varieties.

White

Chardonnay: Colour from pale to straw gold. Aroma can evoke peach, pineapple, sweet apple. Flavours of sweet apple, with creaminess or toffee from oak contact.

Fiano: Italian variety said to have been cultivated from ancient Roman times in Campania region of southern Italy. Now widely planted on the mainland and in Sicily, it makes dry but soft wines of colours ranging from pale to pure gold with aromas of honey, orchard fruit, almonds and candied apricot. Well-made examples have beautifully balanced nutty-fresh flavours. Fiano is becoming deeply fashionable.

Pinot Grigio: In its home territory of north-east Italy, it makes wines of pale colour, and pale flavour too. What makes the wine so popular might well be its natural low acidity. Better wines are more aromatic, even smoky, and pleasingly weighty in the manner of the Pinot Gris made in Alsace.

Riesling: In German wines, pale colour, sharp-apple aroma, racy fruit whether dry or sweet. Faint spritz common in young wines. Petrolly hint in older wines. Australian and New Zealand Rieslings have more colour and weight, and often a minerally, limey twang.

Sauvignon Blanc: In the dry wines, pale colour with suggestion of green. Aromas of asparagus, gooseberries, nettles, seagrass. Green, grassy fruit.

Semillon: Colour can be rich yellow. Aromas of tropical fruit including pineapple and bananas. Even in dry wines, hints of honey amid fresh, fruit-salad flavours.

Viognier: Intense pale-gold colour. Aroma evokes apricots, blanched almonds and fruit blossom. Flavours include candied fruits. Finish often low in acidity.

Red

Cabernet Sauvignon: Dense colour, purple in youth. Strong aroma of blackcurrants and cedar wood ('cigar box'). Flavour concentrated, often edged with tannin so it grips the mouth.

Grenache: Best known in the Côtes du Rhône, it tends to make red wines pale in colour but forceful in flavour with a wild, hedgerow-fruit style and hints of pepper.

Merlot: Dark, rich colour. Aroma of sweet black cherry. Plummy, rich, mellow fruit can be akin to Cabernet but with less tannin. May be hints of bitter chocolate.

Pinot Noir: Colour distinctly pale, browning with age. Aromas of strawberry and raspberry. Light-bodied wine with soft-fruit flavours but dry, clean finish.

Sangiovese: The grape of Chianti and now of several other Italian regions, too. Colour is fine ruby, and may be relatively light; a plummy or even pruny smell is typical and flavours can evoke blackcurrant, raspberry and nectarine. Tannin lingers, so the wine will have a dry, nutskin-like finish.

Shiraz or Syrah: Intense, near-black colour. Aroma of ripe fruit, sometimes spicy. Robust, rich flavours, commonly with high alcohol, but with soft tannins. The Shiraz of Australia is typically much more substantial than the Syrah of the south of France.

Tempranillo: Colour can be pale, as in Rioja. Blackcurrant aroma, often accompanied by vanilla from oak ageing. Tobacco, even leather, evoked in flavours.

There is more about all these varieties, and many others, in 'What wine words mean' starting on page 123.

My top
—*supermarket wines*—

First, a short explanation of my scoring system. As an entirely subjective guide to relative value among the wines mentioned in the book, I use a scoring scale of 0 to 10. In the notes I take while tasting, I give each wine a score within this range, and most of the wines I have given a score of 8 and above are included. Wines scoring 7 and under are almost entirely left out, because this is not a book in which there is space to decry wines I have not liked.

I do recommend all the wines mentioned. If they score 6 or 7, it means I have liked the wine but have doubts about the price, or believe that while the wine is not entirely to my own taste, I can see it might appeal to others. A score of 8 signifies a very good wine at a fair price and a score of 9 indicates special quality and value. Those that earn 10 out of 10 are, obviously enough, the wines I don't think can be bettered.

Out of the 2,000-or-so supermarket wines I have tasted over the year, 28 scored the maximum 10 out of 10. Listed on pages 24 and 25, the still wines range in price from about £3 to £13, which I hope provides reassurance that there are great wines for every kind of budget. Among the top-scoring wines, the honours are fairly well spread. Nation by nation, France is a clear first with nine, followed by Spain on five. Australia has four, Argentina and Italy three, and there is one apiece for Chile, Germany, New Zealand and South Africa.

Supermarket of the year in these terms goes rather awkwardly to Majestic, which isn't a supermarket at all, but has six wines scoring 10. Next is a surprise runner-up, the Co-op, with five top-scorers. It's all happening at the Co-op as the vast network of more than 3,000 licensed stores extends its food and drink range ever wider and more upmarket – and in numbers, too, with the takeover of Somerfield's 800 branches. Tesco and Waitrose tie with four top wines, and are followed by Marks & Spencer with three and Asda, Booths and Sainsbury's with two.

On a more rational basis, I must nominate Waitrose as the best supermarket in which to shop for wine. The diversity is astounding, they have an excellent website and home-delivery service, endless discounts, and a wonderful range of 'fine' wines. And in spite of the general belief that the stores are more expensive than those of its rivals, wine prices at Waitrose are fully competitive, and they have a terrific range of cheaper bottles. Waitrose has six wines among my pick of the 20 best bargains under £4 – more than any other retailer.

The Co-op and Asda are both improving fast, Sainsbury's is standing still and Morrisons – wine-wise – is moribund. Tesco never fails to impress – the website and Wine Club are easy to get on with – and I can say exactly the same about Marks & Spencer. Booths, the Lancashire chain to which most of us can get access only via mail order, has whizzed up its website in 2009, and it is easier than ever to get at the entire, marvellous range of wines.

Some names are not here. Aldi and Lidl, the German twins doing so well with their discounts in the downturn, are omitted because neither offers any assistance to journalists like me who seek to write up their wines. In the absence of invitations to tastings or any kind of range information, I have bought a number of bottles from both chains I thought might deliver the sort of value that is so convincingly represented by their respective food offerings. But there is nothing positive to report, I am sad to say.

Also absent is Somerfield. It was confirmed early in 2009 that the Co-op is to take over the Bristol-based chain and the name will disappear completely from the high streets, where most of its 800-plus stores are located, by 2011. The nice wine team at the Co-op tell me it is too early to say whether any of the stalwart Somerfield wine brands will be carried over into the Co-op range, but I rather doubt it. I will miss the excellent Prince William champagnes, but not much else, I fear.

A last word on alcohol levels and vintages. In the descriptions of the wines I have mentioned these where they are notably high or low. Any wine with 14 per cent or more alcohol by volume is noted, as is any with less than 12 per cent alcohol by volume. For readers to whom such information matters, I hope this is of some help.

If no vintage date is appended to the name in the listings, the wine is 'non-vintage', meaning it is a blend of wines made from two or more different harvests. This is quite usual for cheap wines, and little significance need be attached to it except in dry white wines, where the principle of the newer, the better usually applies. Most whites are past their freshest within their first year, so buying them when they are older, in whole or part, might be a tad risky.

The Top-Scoring Wines of the Year

Twenty-eight wines score 10 out of 10 for quality, excitement and value for 2010: 14 reds, 12 whites, 2 sparklers – and no rosés.

Red wines

Siciliano Rosso 2008	£3.23	Tesco
Gamay Vin de Pays d'Ardèche 2008	£3.99	Marks & Spencer
Jumilla Finca La Solana Monastrell 2007	£4.99	Co-op
La Grille Pinot Noir 2007	£5.99	Majestic
Taste the Difference Malbec 2007	£5.99	Sainsbury's
Finest Valpolicella Ripasso 2006	£6.14	Tesco
Co-op Fairtrade Organic Argentine Malbec Reserva 2008	£6.49	Co-op
Weinert Carrascal 2005	£6.99	Majestic
Barón de Ley Club Privado Reserva Rioja 2005	£7.99	Waitrose
Château d'Argadens 2004	£7.99	Booths
Finest St Emilion 2007	£8.98	Tesco
Gulf Station Pinot Noir 2008	£9.99	Sainsbury's
Gigondas Domaine de Nôtre Dames des Pallières 2006	£11.99	Majestic
Les Mines Bellmunt del Priorat 2006	£12.99	Marks & Spencer

White wines

Gran Tesoro Viura 2008	£3.49	Tesco
Virtue Sauvignon Blanc/ Chardonnay 2008	£3.99	Waitrose
River 216 Gewürztraminer-Riesling 2008	£4.99	Co-op
De Bortoli Verdelho 2008	£5.99	Waitrose

Tre Cupole Grillo 2008	£5.99	Majestic
Palatia Pinot Grigio 2008	£6.99	Marks & Spencer
Explorers Vineyard Sauvignon Blanc 2008	£7.49	Co-op
Extra Special Clare Valley Riesling 2008	£7.98	Asda
Valençay Le Clos du Château Claude Lafond 2008	£7.99	Majestic
Jordan Estate Chardonnay 2007	£9.99	Booths
Rias Baixas Albariño Martin Codax 2008	£10.99	Majestic
Château Roumier Sauternes 2006	£11.99	Co-op

Sparkling wines

Crémant de Bourgogne Cave de Lugny Blanc de Blancs	£9.99	Waitrose
Extra Special Vintage Champagne 2002	£19.98	Asda

Budget-conscious wines

All the retailers are striving to stock decent bottles at affordable prices for the many customers struggling to cope in the present vicious downturn. Here are my top ten reds, and whites with rosés, under the £4 threshold. Do remember that in any wine priced at under £4, more than half what you pay goes to the Treasury in excise duty and VAT.

Top Ten Reds Under £4

Siciliano Rosso 2008	£3.23	Tesco
Asda Syrah Vin de Pays d'Oc 2008	£3.28	Asda
Tesco Claret	£3.38	Tesco
Cuvée Chasseur 2008	£3.69	Waitrose

Gran Tesoro Garnacha 2007	£3.89	Booths
Classic Côtes du Rhône 2008	£3.99	Waitrose
Gamay Vin de Pays d'Ardèche 2008	£3.99	Marks & Spencer
Le Chiave Montepulciano d'Abruzzo 2008	£3.99	Co-op
Sainsbury's Beaujolais	£3.99	Sainsbury's
Virtue Merlot/Cabernet Sauvignon 2008	£3.99	Waitrose

Top Ten Whites and Rosés Under £4

Asda Smart Price South African White	£2.98	Asda
Asda Marsanne Vin de Pays d'Oc 2008	£3.28	Asda
Vieille Fontaine Vin de Pays d'Oc 2008	£3.29	Tesco
Gran Tesoro Viura 2008	£3.49	Tesco
Cuvée Fleur Rosé 2008	£3.79	Waitrose
Asda Pinot Grigio 2008	£3.98	Asda
Las Falleras Rosé 2008	£3.99	Marks & Spencer
The Co-operative Frascati 2007	£3.99	Co-op
Trinacria Bianco 2008	£3.99	Waitrose
Virtue Sauvignon Blanc/ Chardonnay 2008	£3.99	Waitrose

Asda

Asda is hardly a Cinderella among supermarkets – only Tesco is bigger – but as a wine retailer, the Wal-Mart-owned chain's 356 stores have not exactly been at the forefront for quality, choice, or even noticeably for value. Until the last couple of years, that is. In the summer of 2009 I went to taste more than a hundred of the new Asda wines, and was greatly impressed. The own-label range in particular is now fit to rival any of the competition. The experts agree. 'We have won more medals for our own-labels than any other supermarket in this year's industry awards, the International Wine Challenge, Decanter World Wine Awards and International Wine and Spirit Competition,' says Master of Wine Philippa Carr, who runs the Asda wine department.

It shows. Highlights included wine from the Asda Smart Price range, all priced below £3, and including thoroughly respectable wines from South Africa and Italy. Among the standard own-label range, there are very sound vins de pays at not-much-over £3 and some true bargains from Italy too.

There is more excitement among the 'Extra Special' range. The Chablis Domaine de la Levée 2007 at £8.98 is a stand-out wine, and the Châteauneuf du Pape 2007 at £11.98 likewise. The Clare Valley Riesling 2008 (£7.98) is superb, and the Extra Special Vintage Champagne 2002 (£19.98) is my bargain champagne of the year.

RED WINES

asda

ARGENTINA

8 Asda Argentinian Malbec 2008   £3.98
Grippy but not tough, an easy-drinking dark-fruit food red – try with shepherd's pie.

8 Vinalba Malbec Syrah 2006   £6.83
Nicely oaked and moderated mature blend has the robust leather whiff of the Malbec and the silk and spice of the Syrah.

AUSTRALIA

**9 Extra Special Coonawarra
Cabernet Sauvignon 2005**   £6.98
Looks like blood, but runs smooth and silky with a beckoning sweet nose, hint of toffee, lush ripe blackcurranty fruit and 14% alcohol. A real comfort, made by Katnook.

7 Extra Special McLaren Vale Shiraz 2007   £6.98
Jumbo soupy chilli-chocolate fruit bomb for manly thirsts to match highly flavoured meat dishes; 14.5% alcohol.

CHILE

7 Asda Chilean Cabernet Sauvignon 2008   £3.11
Looked at in the light of its price, a good wine because it is drinkable: blackcurrants with a caramel note.

FRANCE

9 Asda Syrah Vin de Pays d'Oc 2008   £3.28
Deep purple, sweetly friendly and natural-tasting spicy dry-finishing honest food red (beany stews) at an unbelievable price.

9 Extra Special Beaujolais Villages 2007   £4.61
This jumped out, because it is the juicy, bouncing essence of what Beaujolais should be. Wildly fruity nose and purple-squishy flavours that grip the taste buds.

RED WINES

FRANCE

9   **Extra Special Côtes du Rhône**
     Villages 2007   **£4.74**
So ripe it's almost scorched, a grippingly good plum-and-peppery food wine at a bargain price.

8   **Extra Special Merlot 2008**   **£5.98**
Black cherry fruit with a bitter-chocolate centre in this muscular vin de pays d'Oc to match meaty dishes.

8   **Extra Special Shiraz 2008**   **£5.98**
A vin de pays d'Oc labelled Shiraz (the Aussie name) instead of indigenous Syrah, but a well-made, enriched blackberry, peppery red of character.

8   **Paul Mas La Forge Estate**
     Cabernet Sauvignon 2008   **£6.98**
Inky maroon New-World-style Languedoc heavyweight has intense plummy fruit, hint of mint. Plush.

8   **Vacqueyras 2006**   **£7.24**
Nicely rounded and weighty Rhône with dark, spicy fruit and 14% alcohol.

9   **Cellier des Dauphins Côtes du Rhône**
     Villages Vinsobres 2007   **£8.98**
Under a brand known more for value than interest, this is a very proper wine, dense and gripping, with 14% alcohol with both pepper and lush ripeness.

8   **Extra Special Châteauneuf du Pape**
     2007   **£11.98**
Rare bird this, as it is (by supermarket Châteauneuf standards) approachable in both condition and price. Nice mélange of dark fruit, mellow and savoury, 14.5% alcohol.

RED WINES

Asda (sidebar)

ITALY

🍷 8 **Asda Valpolicella 2008**   £3.47
Cherry-ripe, almondy sweet but not sugary, correct dry finish, to drink cool.

🍷 8 **Asda Chianti 2007**   £3.78
Cheap drinkable Chianti is rare; this has authentic cherry-nutty style, is dry but not dried out, lively and stimulating.

🍷 8 **Extra Special Valpolicella Ripasso 2007**   £6.18
Delicious reinforced Valpolicella has dark fruit with coffee and cinnamon notes, long flavours, agreeable nutty dryness. Great cheese wine.

🍷 8 **Extra Special Chianti Classico Riserva 2005** £7.20
Nice fleshy bright-fruit nutty-finishing proper Chianti; this vintage is much better than the 2004 that might also be on the shelf.

N ZEALAND

🍷 9 **Extra Special New Zealand
        Pinot Noir 2008**   £8.98
Pale but intensely raspberry-fruit, smoothly oaked classic Pinot by ace Wither Hills winery has keen citrus top note. Lovely stuff, it seems cheap.

SOUTH AFRICA

🍷 8 **Asda Smart Price South African Red**   £2.98
Bright and juicy but substantial cheapo from Cinsault and Pinotage grapes.

🍷 8 **Asda South African Pinotage 2008**   £3.78
Ripe, savoury, toasty typical Pinotage with plenty of welly (14% alcohol).

RED WINES

S AFRICA

♟9 **Hopes Garden Cabernet Sauvignon 2007** £4.48
Really impressive Fairtrade wine of sunny disposition:
pure briary flavours, touch of oaky richness, healthy
balance, 14% alcohol, and jolly cheap.

SPAIN

♟7 **Asda Marques del Norte Rioja 2007** £3.98
Light but firmly fruity youthful Rioja to drink cool.

♟8 **Tiers II Rioja Crianza 2005** £5.88
Cigar-box nose and vanilla richness identify this
traditional Rioja with healthy, long fruit.

♟8 **The Pilgrimage Mazuelo 2007** £6.12
Gutsy, thoroughly Spanish dark sleek red for food (try
paella) with mint and spice and 14% alcohol.

♟9 **Tiers III Rioja Reserva 2005** £6.88
Long-aged wine has an alluring orange-brown colour,
coffee, cedar whiff and delicate but rich flavours. Good
price for such an elegant old thing.

PINK WINES

ITALY

♟7 **Asda Smart Price Seven Hills Rosé** £2.97
Light, dry party pink with modest 11% alcohol shows
cherry-raspberry style of constituent Sangiovese grapes.

SPAIN

♟7 **Pleyades Garnacha Rosada 2008** £4.97
Strongly coloured and perfumed pink has a rose-hip
nuance; finishes dry though.

WHITE WINES

Asda

ARGENTINA

8 **Asda Argentinian Torrontes 2008** £4.30
Pleasing Muscatty dry refresher from Argentina's native white grape. Aperitif or with Asian food.

AUSTRALIA

9 **Ken Forrester The Coolest Cape Chenin Blanc Semillon 2007** £6.22
Sounds complicated, but this big yellow tropical-fruit dry food wine (chicken or fish) has easy charm. Great limey edge and 14% alcohol.

8 **Zilzie Viognier 2008** £6.78
One of numerous Viogniers (now a rather passé variety, I'd thought) shown by Asda, this Murray Darling version is big, plump (14.5% alcohol) and bursting with exotic candied-fruit flavours, finishing brisk and tangy. Lovely aperitif.

10 **Extra Special Clare Valley Riesling 2008** £7.98
This really is extra special, a succulent, powerful Riesling constructed on a nectarine model – wildly fruity with ideal acidity. It is made by excellent winery Knappstein.

FRANCE

9 **Asda Marsanne Vin de Pays d'Oc 2008** £3.28
Bland label won't sell this likeable wine, but the price will help; it has a distinctive almondy-apricot richness balancing the keen crispness of flavour.

8 **Extra Special Viognier 2008** £5.98
Proper marrowy candied-apricot style to this big, ripe Languedoc Viognier, nicely finished with citrus edge.

WHITE WINES

FRANCE

 **Bouchard Vin de Pays d'Oc Chardonnay
2007** £6.08
Lushly ripe burgundy-style (but unoaked) Mediterranean
dry white with nice balance of sweet-apple fruit and crisp
minerality.

 Extra Special Gewürztraminer 2007 £6.98
Luscious lychee perfume and corresponding fruit from
this grand Alsace wine made by an unfamiliar but jolly-
sounding producer, Cave de Roi Dagobert.

 Chablis Domaine de la Levée 2007 £8.98
Immediately identifiable stony-fresh example of the great
burgundy appellation. Lovely Chardonnay expression,
and it's Chablis all the way.

ITALY

 Asda Pinot Grigio 2008 £3.98
From Adige Valley in sub-Alpine Italy and made by giant
Cavit, a very likeable bright, crunchy, spicy PG with real
fruit impact. Great value.

Asda Soave Classico 2008 £4.03
Lively green-fruit style with an endearing blanched-
almond note, this is only 50p more than the basic Asda
Soave, and twice as good.

Extra Special Fiano 2008 £5.97
Well-coloured aromatic and crisp-finishing, but by Fiano
standards, not all that special, especially at the price.

WHITE WINES

NEW ZEALAND

8 **Asda New Zealand Sauvignon Blanc 2008** £5.47
Nettly aroma and matching fruit with added gooseberry
and seagrass; soft finish. Commercial, and decent value.

8 **Southbank Estate Marlborough**
Sauvignon Blanc 2008 £7.98
Great whiff of asparagus and waves of lively lush
seagrass fruit and freshness.

SOUTH AFRICA

8 **Asda Smart Price South African White** £2.98
An innocent bargain, blended from Colombard, Chenin
Blanc and Chardonnay, it's dry but soft, insouciant,
healthy – and cheap.

Sparkling Wines

AUSTRALIA

🍷8   **Griffith Park Sparkling Brut**   £6.98
Impressive dry, vigorous sparkler from Chardonnay and
Pinot Noir grapes (the champagne formula) has toasty
whiff and fresh orchard fruit.

FRANCE

🍷9   **Asda Champagne Brut**   £14.03
Generously coloured, bready nosed and ripely fruity (nice
apple twang), a proper champagne by Nicolas Feuillatte.
Bargain.

🍷10   **Extra Special Vintage Champagne 2002**   £19.98
As a consoling celebration wine, this fits. Though below
£20 it has all the attributes of vintage champagne:
enticing gold colour; rounded, brioche aromas; long,
luxurious and soothing flavours.

ITALY

🍷8   **Extra Special Prosecco Rosé**   £6.98
Soft rather than sweet, a brightly hued and breezily fruity
Veneto fizz well above average for interest and freshness.

SPAIN

🍷9   **Extra Special Cava Vintage 2005**   £5.98
I must confess to a chronic sniffiness about cava, but this
one jumped out of the crowd; with full orchard-fruit
flavours and mellow maturity, my favourite cava of the
year at a bargain price.

Booths

This family-owned company, founded in 1847, well before any of the better-known chains, has just 26 supermarkets, all in north-west England. The company is much admired in its own region, and from afar by southerners like me for its impeccably chosen wine range which is, thank goodness, available in its entirety online. The website is clear and simple to operate. Much improved and updated in 2009, it is easy to follow and to order from.

Rather unexpectedly, Booths operates the most comprehensive wine-selling website in Britain. Launched ten years ago, **www.everywine.co.uk** is a by-the-case service that lists about 40,000 different wines. It's not that all of these wines are in the company's modest warehouse, but the clever chap who runs the site with his small team, Rob Pearce, knows exactly where to find them. Prices, always per case of 6 or 12, are quoted on the site.

All the wines sold in Booths supermarkets can also be bought on the **everywine** website, but you don't have to buy them a case at a time – you're free to order a single bottle if you choose, or mix your own case of a dozen different wines. A new feature is special-offer cases of pre-mixed dozens at useful discounts.

Booths have an uncanny knack of not just providing excellent everyday wines at canny prices, but picking out really outstanding names for the more upmarket categories. Their champagnes, for example, include the little-known but simply wonderful H Blin, which I have never seen in any other supermarket. They have a proper range of German wines, and as I never tire of banging on about, they have the only real, dry, red and ridiculously delicious Lambrusco that you can buy (as far as I know), anywhere in Britain. And so on.

For those not fortunate enough to live within, say, an hour's travel of a Booths store, do log on to **www.everywine.co.uk** for the full picture. Based on my own experience, delivery is very prompt – four working days for my cases – and the charge is £5.95 whatever the size of your order (including a single bottle), and wherever you live on the mainland. For those not much good at computers, you can ring 0800 072 0011 to place orders. Booths publish a list of wines around Christmas time, which makes a very informative and tempting read, including lots of special offers. You could phone up and ask for a copy.

RED WINES

8 **Réserve du Reverend Corbières 2005** £4.99
Dark, gripping and peppery food wine (pork and/or beans) from a very ripe and now mellow vintage.

9 **Paul Jaboulet Aîné Parallèle 45 2006** £7.59
Fabulous mature vintage of this very respectable Côtes du Rhône brand from a great producer.

8 **St Joseph Cave de St Désirat 2006** £7.99
Fine, silky, northern-Rhône mature Syrah has warming black fruit and spice.

10 **Château D'Argadens 2004** £7.99
Lovely cedary-silky, rounded but structured claret from 12th-century château ranked a humble 'Bordeaux Superieur' but owned by Sichel of Château Palmer fame.

8 **Château Pey La Tour 2006** £9.99
Robust new-style claret with upfront fruit (95% Merlot) has black-cherry ripeness, long flavours and a grip of tannin. Will keep.

8 **Château Preuillac 2002** £12.99
It was £10.99 a year ago, but this silky Médoc is, in fairness, impoving with time: plumply ripe with keen black fruit, a classic claret.

8 **Tenuta al Sole Negroamaro 2006** £4.99
Big Salento red balances sweet briar flavours with a mouth-wringing dark tannic grip. Good pasta match.

FRANCE

ITALY

RED WINES

ITALY

🍷**9** **Cantine Due Palme Rosso Salentino 2006** £5.99
Insinuating plump blackberry-fruit oak-enriched wine with an agreeably surprising dry, nutty finish. So well made.

🍷**8** **1489 Vino Nobile di Montepulciano 2005** £9.99
Dark, minty and exotically spiced de luxe Tuscan Sangiovese has sinewy plum fruit, vanilla richness, long flavours.

N ZEALAND

🍷**8** **Mud House Pinot Noir 2007** £8.99
Sleek raspberry-ripe discreetly earthy Marlborough Pinot is likeable and well-priced.

SPAIN

🍷**8** **Gran Tesoro Garnacha 2007** £3.89
Dark and juicy, characteristically Spanish party red with a keen, spicy finish.

PINK WINES

FRANCE

🍷**8** **Louis Jadot Beaujolais Rosé 2007** £8.99
Novelty wine, but really very jolly with its glowing colour, raspberry nose and juicy redcurrant fruit.

WHITE WINES

AUSTRALIA

9 **Brown Brothers Dry Muscat Blanc 2007** £5.49
It really is dry, but it is also grapy with honey traces and hints of fresh pineapple, ginger, lychees and nectarine. A marvel.

8 **D'Arenberg The Hermit Crab
Viognier/Marsanne 2008** £8.69
Terrific amalgam of flavours in this dry but exotic McLaren Vale blend. Contrives to be both rich and crisp.

FRANCE

8 **Mâcon Villages Cave de Lugny
Chardonnay 2007** £6.49
Nifty mineral southern burgundy has racy but peachy fruit. True to its origins.

GERMANY

9 **Gau-Bickelheimer Kürfurstenstück
Auslese 2007** £4.99
Not a Riesling, so it's cheap, but a lovely honeyed Rheinhessen aperitif wine with gold colour, ripe autumnal fruit, mineral freshness and just 10% alcohol.

8 **Louis Gunthrum Riesling 2008** £5.99
Straight racy Rheinhessen QbA is craftily soft rather than sweet – a fine, delicate aperitif.

9 **Villa Wolf Pinot Gris 2007** £6.99
One of the Rhine's most inventive wines, from Ernie Loosen, this is aromatic, richly coloured and brimming with lush, smoky, herbaceous flavours.

ITALY

8 **A Mano Fiano Greco 2007** £6.99
Artful balance of candied-fruit and keen (grapefruit?) tang in this Puglian dry white is a treat. Look out too for the 2008.

WHITE WINES

ITALY

🍷**9** **Pieropan Soave Classico 2007**   £9.99
The definitive Soave with the perfect expression of racy, vegetal fruit and thrilling citrus acidity.

PORTUGAL

🍷**8** **Quinta de Azevedo Vinho Verde 2008**   £5.99
Tangy, crisp and citrussy authentic Minho wine is a great match for mackerel or sardines and just 10.5% alcohol.

S AFRICA

🍷**10** **Jordan Estate Chardonnay 2007**   £9.99
Maybe it's just me, but the Jordan family of Stellenbosch seem to make the most natural, comprehensible, oaked pure-fruit Chardonnay in the world. At ten quid a go, all enthusiasts can afford to test my view.

SPAIN

🍷**8** **Torres Viña Esmeralda 2008**   £7.49
Intriguing Catalan aperitif dry white from Muscat and Gewürztraminer abounds with tropical flavours, finishing limey crisp.

SPARKLING WINES

FRANCE

🍷**8** **H Blin Champagne Brut 2002**   £23.99
Lovely maturing biscuity and complex champagne you won't find in other supermarkets; price has lifted somewhat from last year's £19.99.

ITALY

🍷**9** **Medici Concerto Lambrusco 2007**   £7.99
This is real Lambrusco, inky red, busily fizzy, bursting with sweet cherry-brambly fruit, eagerly stimulating and refreshing, finishes very dry.

Co-op

The Co-op just grows and grows. It has more than 3,000 licensed food outlets, most of which have been transformed over the last couple of years from utilitarian convenience shops to shiny supermarket-style stores with an increasingly upmarket range of products.

This includes the wines. In 2009 there were some seriously good additions from Australia and New Zealand, and at two tastings I was mighty impressed with the Fairtrade wines from Latin America. The Co-op deserves recognition as the leading retailer of Fairtrade wines, and its policy of detailing every ingredient in all of its own-label wines is also a very worthy one. No other retailer does this, yet.

Looking back at my notes, I was quite surprised to discover that I had scored 5 out of only about 50 wines tasted at a maximum 10 out of 10. This is more than at any other supermarket, including those at which I have tasted up to 300 wines. I think it speaks volumes about the quiet, methodical improvements taking place at the Co-op, and it bodes well for the future.

RED WINES

ARGENTINA

8 **Co-op Argentine Malbec 2007** £4.29
Previous vintages have been hard, but this is mellow, savoury and intense with minty-blackberry juiciness.

10 **Co-op Fairtrade Organic Argentine
Malbec Reserva 2008** £6.49
This has everything as well as PC credentials: massive purple colour; leafy, rich leather-upholstered nose; dense ripe chocolate-centred black-fruit flavours with a caramel note but elegant weight; grapefruit twang of acidity.

AUSTRALIA

9 **River 216 Shiraz-Petite Sirah 2008** £4.99
Plump brambly fruit is nicely rounded with a firm grip; long, intense and satisfying.

8 **Cellar 150 Shiraz 2007** £7.99
Dense, hugely ripe (14.5% alcohol) McLaren Vale is just short of syrupy and really rather poised. Has been down to £4.99.

8 **Yalumba Barossa Shiraz-Viognier 2006** £8.99
Blood-coloured roasty-spicy oaked smoothie is given a tropical lift by the splash of Viognier (14% alcohol).

9 **D'Arry's Original Grenache-Shiraz 2006** £9.99
Special-occasion McLaren Vale monster (14.5% alcohol) has perfume of roses and redcurrant and rich black fruit with a white-pepper lift. Needs meat.

CHILE

8 **Chilean Fairtrade Carmenère 2008** £4.99
Strong raspberry perfume, buttered-toast nose and eager, clingy blackcurrant fruit.

RED WINES

CHILE

8   **Carmen Merlot Reserva 2006**   £8.99
Casablanca claret: elegant rather than upfront (though 14.5% alcohol) luxury red of obvious class.

FRANCE

8   **Palais des Anciens Côtes du Rhône**
      Réserve 2006   £6.99
Big but light on its feet, a healthy red with spicy Mediterranean flavours and grippy finish.

8   **Domaine Brisson Morgon**
      Les Charmes 2006   £7.99
Juicy mature Beaujolais with firm, healthy fruit. A real find.

8   **Château Sissan Grande Réserve 2006**   £8.99
Dense purple and tannic Bordeaux is bursting with fruit; makes an immediate impression and will develop for a couple more years.

ITALY

9   **Le Chiave Montepulciano d'Abruzzo 2008**   £3.99
Jolly, bouncing and brambly mauve-coloured dry-edged pasta wine has a real gush of fruit. Cheap.

SPAIN

10   **Finca la Solana Monastrell 2007**   £4.99
From Jumilla-Valencia a huge, opaque, plumptiously ripe 14%-alcohol red with cherry and chocolate notes leading to a lovely dry edge. Co-op buyer Ben Cahill suggests decanting a day before drinking.

9   **El Mesón Rioja Crianza 2005**   £8.99
Look out for this one on offer at £4.99; it is lush with raspberry fruit, creamy and long.

Red Wines

8 **Cycles Gladiator Pinot Noir 2006** £7.49

From California's Central Coast, an elegant earthy-cherry-raspberry wine with silky appeal; don't be put off by the weird presentation.

USA

Pink Wines

9 **Fairtrade Malbec Rosé 2008** £4.99

Nice onion-skin colour, crisp bramble-strawberry flavours that linger but finish brisk and clean.

ARGENTINA

White Wines

 8 **The Co-operative Lime Tree Pinot Grigio 2008** £4.75

Did I taste lime zest? A likeable fresh Aussie spin on an Italian favourite.

10 **River 216 Gewürztraminer-Riesling 2008** £4.99

Gold colour, tropical-herbaceous aroma and fruit with a crisp green lift at the finish. A distinctively delicious aperitif at a most unusually sensible price.

 8 **D'Arenberg Broken Fishplate Sauvignon Blanc 2008** £8.99

Strong asparagus note to an exuberantly fruity seagrass-fresh Adelaide wine with long, long flavours.

AUSTRALIA

8 **Knappstein Gewürztraminer-Riesling-Pinot Grigio 2008** £8.99

Dense and exotic in the Alsace style with keen limey edge; fresh and long.

WHITE WINES

CHILE

8 **Errazuriz Wild Ferment Chardonnay 2007** **£8.99**
Rich gold wine in every sense; opulent but not overblown.

FRANCE

8 **Les Jamelles Viognier 2008** **£5.79**
Mellow and plump Languedoc dry white has authentic apricot richness and a clean edge.

10 **Château Roumier Sauternes 2006 37.5cl** **£11.99**
Ambrosial Sauternes perfectly balanced between succulent, honeyed richness and fleetingly limey acidity ensuring its flavours linger, but do not cloy. Even at full price, a bargain, but the Co-op has been known to discount by half.

ITALY

9 **The Co-operative Frascati 2007** **£3.99**
Nice tight fruit in this brisk, fresh Roman classic with a lemon twang. Surprise.

7 **The Co-operative Veneto Pinot Grigio 2008** **£4.99**
Marzipan nose, clean fruit and a plumpness perhaps down to the 15% added Chardonnay.

NEW ZEALAND

7 **Five Hills Pinot Grigio 2008** **£5.99**
Brisk pebbly refresher with little resemblance to Pinot Grigio style (and maybe none the worse for that).

10 **Explorers Vineyard Sauvignon Blanc 2008** **£7.49**
This hits the spot, an exhilaratingly fresh and zingy wine with sea-grass aroma, tinglingly gooseberry-nettle fruit and a luxuriously long finish. Outstanding value at the price.

WHITE WINES

NEW ZEALAND

🍷8 **Tawhiri Sauvignon Blanc 2008**   £7.99
Wild label, and the animated asparagus-lime flavours live up to it.

🍷8 **The Co-operative Marlborough
Pinot Grigio 2008**   £7.99
Exotic, Alsace-like whiff and fruit from this smoky-spicy-fleshy PG to relish with food – especially Asian.

S AFRICA

🍷7 **Ashwood Chardonnay Chenin Blanc**   £7.99
Leafy-crisp and fresh with a lick of sweetness. Look out for this charmer on promo at half price.

USA

🍷7 **The Boulders Pinot Grigio Reserve 2008**   £5.99
Enormously fruity peachy-spicy food wine will stand up to anything.

SPARKLING WINES

FRANCE

🍷9 **Le Drappier Champagne Brut**   £19.99
Lemon-gold colour, yeasty-bready aroma and full, wholesome flavours suggesting plenty of bottle age. Look out for regular discounts on this excellent champagne.

Majestic

 Majestic is a marvel. They persist with traditional wines the supermarkets now largely disdain: a real choice from Beaujolais and the Loire, ambitious burgundies at realistic prices (by burgundy standards anyway), a new range of good sherries, impressive inexpensive white wines from Chile. You name it.

And they persist too with discounting on an epic scale, so that the list prices, as faithfully transcribed here, are largely an irrelevance, because so many of these wines, on the day you drop into a branch or look online, will be on sale at a discount of at least 20 per cent.

Champagne and sparkling wines are the most bewildering. They are all on permanent special offers based on the principle of buy 2 bottles, get a discount of anywhere between 20 and 50 per cent. The single-bottle prices look like a leg-pull, mind you. Who in their right mind would pay £39.99 for a Pol Roger Brut non-vintage? On the other hand, buy two at £23.99 (that's a 40 per cent discount) and you're paying what this wonderful champagne cost ten years ago.

Yes, I know Majestic is not a supermarket. But in a guide like this, I cannot omit such a major national chain. Unlike other high street merchants (an endangered species in these difficult times), there is always free parking, you get a trolley to put your shopping in, and the person behind the counter will carry your purchases to your car for you.

In my experience, the staff in Majestic are not only strong of arm but also very well qualified to give advice to customers. Most have done demanding wine-education courses, and all seem invariably enthusiastic as well as knowledgeable about the wines stocked. Lazy or indecisive shoppers could leave the whole choice to the staff if they were so minded.

The network of branches has spread dramatically in recent years to a total of 150 from one end of the country (Inverness) to the other (Exeter). But to buy the wines, you need not even stir. Four or five times a year the chain publishes a new, comprehensive price list which you can peruse at home, then simply phone your nearest branch (all the locations and phone numbers are in the list) and order for delivery to your home at no extra charge. If you prefer to order online, **www.majestic.co.uk** is one of the most user-friendly websites in the business.

RED WINES

ARGENTINA

7 Vinalta Malbec 2008 £4.99

Not too much of the toughness to which Argentine Malbecs are prey, with a dark-chocolate centre and 14% alcohol. Some might find it austere, but a good spicy-food red.

10 Weinert Carrascal 2005 £6.99

Bordeaux grape blend is rich and velvety in a Latin way, but elegant in the style of claret too. From one of Argentina's oldest and clearly best producers.

AUSTRALIA

9 Scotchman's Hill Swan Bay Pinot Noir 2007 £8.99

Warmly ripe yet fine-edged silky Pinot of density and length.

9 Kangarilla Road Shiraz 2006 £10.99

Perennial Majestic favourite from McLaren Vale is plump but poised, soft but gently spicy and of a weight that belies its 15% alcohol. Nice botanical label, lovely wine.

CHILE

8 Neblina Merlot 2008 £4.99

Healthily sweet, dark and plummy party plonk.

8 De Martino 347 Vineyards Carmenère Reserva 2007 £7.49

Soft and slinky long-flavoured toasty red with trim finish. Impressive.

9 Carmenère Rucahue Vineyard Lot 21 2007 £9.49

From a great many Chilean wines tasted at Majestic, my favourite. A big blackberry red with 14.5% alcohol and a dark-liquorice heart to the long, slick flavours.

RED WINES

CHILE

🍷 8 **Errazuriz Wild Ferment Pinot Noir 2007**   £10.99
Strong (14.5% alcohol), vivid Casablanca wine of
unusual density but every inch a classic Pinot.

🍷 8 **Cuvée Richard 2008**   £3.79
Straight, ripe southern vin de pays is the same price as
last year, and just as good.

🍷 8 **Beaux Galets 2008**   £3.99
Deeply coloured Merlot-Carignan-Grenache vin de pays
de l'Herault has homely elderberry nose and slurpy
corresponding flavours. Good picnic red.

🍷 10 **Pinot Noir La Grille 2007**   £5.99
Thrillingly eager cherry-ripe Loire wine has a white-
pepper spiciness amid the sweet ripeness. Proper Pinot,
very pale, very interesting.

FRANCE

🍷 8 **Château Marquis de la Grange 2007**   £6.99
Look out for this ripe and sunny claret, especially at
discount to £4.99.

🍷 8 **Domaine Sainte Rose La Garrigue
Syrah Grenache 2007**   £6.99
Nicely weighted (but note 14% alcohol) briary vin de
pays d'Oc claims kin with the 'sweet-smelling thyme and
spicy black pepper of the garrigue'. Fair comment.

🍷 8 **Chénas Louis Chavy 2007**   £8.69
Firmly centred, crisp and juicy flavours in a Beaujolais of
(rarely) classic character.

🍷 7 **Cazal Viel Cuvée des Fées 2007**   £8.99
Muscular Mediterranean red in the distinctive scorched
style of the elusive St Chinian AC.

RED WINES

8 **Beaujolais Lantignié 2008** **£9.99**
Lively almost to the point of prickliness, a joyous purple refresher from Burgundy giant Louis Jadot bodes well for 2008 vintage.

8 **Château l'Ermitage 2000** **£9.99**
Browning, gamey Listrac (Bordeaux) is reassuringly plump and healthy in advancing age.

9 **Château de Gaudou Cuvée**
Renaissance 2005 **£10.99**
Fabulously ripe and intense Cahors needs years to come round, but do invest now. I had a 1999 in 2009, gorgeously rich but still good for another decade.

10 **Gigondas Domaine de Nôtre Dames**
des Pallières 2006 **£11.99**
Big, sinuous and rich wine, 14.5% alcohol, lives up to the good name of this fine Rhône appellation. Quality justifies price.

8 **Chinon Les Varennes du Grand Clos 2004 £14.99**
Rare mature Loire Cabernet Franc has deep maroon colour and deliciously abrading juicy fruit clothed in velvet texture.

9 **Ladoix Domaine Chevalier 2006** **£14.99**
Super silky-earthy classic burgundy Pinot Noir with warm ripeness.

8 **Gevrey-Chambertin Jean Bourguignon**
2006 **£17.99**
Nice complete wine worthy of the famous burgundy appellation.

RED WINES

FRANCE

9 **Nuits St Georges Jean Bourguignon 2006 £17.99**
Crushed-raspberry smell and firm but fleshy corresponding fruit in this lively, long-flavoured burgundy. Lovely wine.

ITALY

8 **Pasqua Sangiovese di Puglia 2007** **£4.99**
Juicy and bright southern party red with clean edge.

9 **Candido I Satiri Salice Salentino**
Riserva 2004 **£8.49**
Colour nearly brown, aroma suggests port and coffee, but the flavour is full of brambly liveliness. Lovely southern food wine.

8 **D'Angelo Sacravite Aglianico 2007** **£9.99**
Spicy volcanic richly fruity southern wine of real interest. A shade pricy but a great treat with meaty pasta recipes.

9 **Vino Nobile di Montepulciano**
La Ciarliana 2004 **£17.99**
Lovely savoury-minty, mature-but-gripping example of this very distinctive de luxe Tuscan wine, with 14% alcohol. Worth the money.

NEW ZEALAND

8 **Villa Maria Cellar Selection**
Pinot Noir 2007 **£12.49**
Kiwi 'burgundy' differs radically in style from the French model, being darker, denser and more plumply sweet variations on the Pinot Noir theme, but they have a charm all their own. This one makes a good intro.

8 **Nautilus Pinot Noir 2007** **£14.99**
Opaque, powerful (14.5% alcohol) Marlborough has massive summer fruit and a tangy lemon acidity.

RED WINES

PORTUGAL

8 **Marco do Pegões 2007** £5.99
Soft but defined blackberry, toasty flavours in this likeable everyday red from southern Terras do Sado region.

S AFRICA

8 **Thelema Cabernet Sauvignon 2005** £22.00
An escapee from Majestic's 'Fine Wine' range, this is one of the Cape's great wines. Still quite tough but gloriously rich and nuanced, invest now but keep it till 2015.

SPAIN

8 **Rioja Gran Reserva Torre Aldea 2001** £11.99
Limpid ruby colour, orange at the rim and a delicate strawberries-and-cream perfume to this supple, luxurious, old-fashioned mature wine. Price has been £8.99.

PINK WINES

8 **La Grille Pinot Noir Rosé 2008** £5.99
Magenta Loire vin de pays has strawberry nose, soft red fruit but crisp finish.

7 **Château Cazal Viel Vieilles Vignes
Rosé 2008** £6.99
Shocking pink, sturdy dry food wine from St Chinian.

8 **Château Guiot Rosé 2008** £6.99
Perennial Costières de Nîmes has strong colour, red-fruit flavours and firm, clean finish.

FRANCE

8 **Château de Sours Rosé 2008** £8.99
Reputable Bordeaux estate's pink has luminous lipstick colour but convincing cherry-cassis fruit and a long, lipsmacking finish.

PINK WINES

N ZEALAND

🍷**9** **Southbank Sauvignon Blanc Rosé 2008** £7.49
Pale salmon colour, distinct Pinot Noir aroma, breezy flavours unmistakably of the Kiwi Sauvignon style, so very crisp and fresh. Deliciously distinct from run-of-the-mill rosé.

PORTUGAL

🍷**7** **Churchill Estates Douro Rosé 2008** £8.99
Magenta wine from the Port vineyards has brisk, crunchy-briary fruit and offers real refreshment.

WHITE WINES

AUSTRALIA

🍷**8** **Coldridge Estate Chardonnay 2007** £4.29
Consistent 'house' Aussie Chardonnay is satisfyingly ripe but perkily fresh. Good price, though now above £4 for the first time.

🍷**8** **Kangarilla Road Chardonnay 2008** £9.99
Lush and long McLaren Vale food wine (shellfish, poultry) is elegantly balanced. I am a sucker for the vine-leaf label.

🍷**9** **Neblina Chardonnay 2008** £4.99
You get a whopping mouthful of peachy-but-mineral fruit for the money. Healthy, balanced party white.

CHILE

🍷**7** **Caliterra Reserva Sauvignon Blanc 2008** £6.24
Tropical-style, low-acidity aperitif wine to please those who don't like their Sauvignon too green.

🍷**9** **Errazuriz Estate Sauvignon Blanc 2008** £6.24
In sharp counterpoint to the Caliterra above, a real gooseberry zinger, fresh, lively – and great value.

White Wines

7 **Galets Blanc 2008** £3.99
Among the shrinking range under £4 at Majestic, this vin de pays d'Oc is soft but refreshing.

8 **La Grille Chenin Blanc,**
Gwenaël Guihard, 2008 £5.99
Dry Anjou wine has a crafty hint of honey with a limey aftertaste. Fine summer aperitif, just 11% alcohol.

8 **Muscadet de Sèvre et Maine Sur Lie**
Domaine de la Tourmaline 2008 £6.49
Bracing but tangily flavoursome rendering of the Loire's classic shellfish matcher.

7 **Bourgogne Chardonnay**
Les Chenaudières 2008 £6.99
From Mâconnais giant Cave de Lugny a yellow, ripe everyday white burgundy at reasonable price (especially with discount).

8 **Domaine Sainte Rose Le Vent du Nord**
Roussanne Chardonnay 2007 £6.99
Plumply rich apple-pie dry vin de pays d'Oc delivers masses of fruit and good balance. Tastes expensive.

7 **Côteaux de Giennois Les Aupières 2008** £7.99
Pebbly-fresh Sauvignon with tangy appeal from a satellite of Pouilly in the Loire. Poor man's Sancerre, but could be cheaper.

10 **Valençay Le Clos du Château,**
Claude Lafond, 2008 £7.99
Lovely intensely lush and grassy Loire Sauvignon with depth and lingering mineral-fresh flavours. Stood out a mile.

WHITE WINES

FRANCE

8 **Bourgogne Chardonnay Louis Jadot 2007** £11.99
Rich but refined style from Burgundy giant Jadot is a safe bet.

8 **Mâcon Milly-Lamartine**
Clos du Four 2008 £11.99
Lush mineral burgundy with wild yellow colour and keen citrus edge.

8 **Meursault Jean Bourguignon 2006** £17.99
Proper sumptuous example of the great Burgundy AC is worthy of the name – and price.

GERMANY

8 **Dr Loosen Riesling Beerenauslese 2006** £9.99
A tiny quarter bottle of Moselle nectar, wickedly honeyed with apple crispness in the background and just 6.8% alcohol. A great treat for elevenses.

8 **Dr Loosen Bernkasteler Badstube**
Riesling Kabinett 2007 £11.99
A new regular Moselle (as distinct from the 'parcel' bargains from Germany that are a major, but fleeting, Majestic feature), this has ripe Granny Smith flavours and just 7.5% alcohol. Lush but not cheap.

ITALY

10 **Tre Cupole Grillo 2008** £5.99
Extraordinary aroma of nectarine and sweet melon in this modern Sicilian wine is followed up by equally bounteous fruit, and capped by impactful citrus acidity.

7 **Verdicchio dei Castelli di Jesi**
Monte Schiavo 2008 £6.99
Crisp, bordering on green, example of this familiar Marches wine. More interesting than most others I have tried.

WHITE WINES

ITALY

🍷8 **Gavi La Lancellotta 2008** £8.74
Has the trademark brassica smell and lots of keen green-herbaceous fruit. Plush food white.

🍷8 **Vernaccia di San Gimignano, Passoni, 2007** £9.99
Attractive lemon-gold colour and heaps of long, grassy fruit in this distinctive and generous Tuscan favourite. Would score higher with a decent discount.

NEW ZEALAND

🍷9 **Marlborough Hills Sauvignon Blanc 2008** £6.24
Keenly priced for a good Kiwi Sauvignon (especially if discounted to £4.99, as it has been), this has a sweet gooseberry smell but zesty fruit. Commercial, and delicious.

🍷8 **Fairleigh Estate Sauvignon Blanc 2008** £6.86
Asparagus dominates in the nose and flavour of this highly distinctive Marlborough aperitif wine.

🍷7 **Villa Maria Cellar Selection
Sauvignon Blanc 2008** £9.99
Nettles and seagrass in this long, soft-finishing top-selling Marlborough brand.

PORTUGAL

🍷8 **Vinho Verde Quinta de Azevedo 2008** £5.99
Well done Majestic for persisting with this no-longer-trendy but deliciously sprightly dry wine with modest alcohol (10.5%) and generous orchardy fruit.

SPAIN

🍷8 **Muga Rioja Blanco 2008** £9.99
Creamy-oaky in the old style of white Rioja, but also brightly fresh in the modern way. A distinctive style.

WHITE WINES

SPAIN

10 **Rias Baixas Albariño Martin Codax 2008** **£10.99**
I thought this seemed expensive until I tasted it. A gorgeously lush green-fruit food wine of huge character, and one of the world's most distinctive styles.

FORTIFIED WINES

SPAIN

8 **Romate Amontillado Sherry** **£6.99**
Fine copper colour, raisiny whiff, dry but with a nutty fruit-cake richness. Drink chilled.

8 **Romate Oloroso Sherry** **£6.99**
A shade darker than the amontillado (above) and a degree stronger at 18% alcohol, this is an elegant, toasted-teacake, dry but richly fruity sherry to take after dinner with cheese. Lovely.

SPARKLING WINES

CHILE

7 **Undurraga Chardonnay Pinot Noir Brut** £9.99
Softly fruity, clean-finishing, and if the buy-2-save-half
deal is on (you pay £4.99), a real bargain.

FRANCE

9 **Pol Roger Brut** £39.99
On top form, creamy, complex and uplifting champagne
of great character and good value if the 40%-off-2-bottles
(price becomes £23.99) offer is prevailing.

ITALY

8 **Prosecco di Conegliano La Marca Cuvée** £14.99
Pale and grapy-smelling, busily foaming and really quite
dry, crisp and refreshing. Buy only on the 2-bottles-save-
a-third deal (£9.99).

N ZEALAND

9 **Lindauer Special Reserve Blanc de Blancs** £11.99
Pick of the day's sparklers, this French-owned Kiwi fizz
has good colour and apple-pie-with-cream lushness. At
buy-2-pay-£6.99, a snip.

USA

7 **Gloria Ferrer Blanc de Noirs** £22.49
It doesn't call itself a rosé, but it has a grey-pink colour
and is really rather elegant and champagne-like. Good at
one-third off if you buy 2 (£14.99).

—Marks & Spencer—

 Strictly speaking, M&S is not a supermarket at all, but it does compete head-on with the grocery giants, in terms of both quality and price. Marks' wines, unlike so many of the food products, don't cost significantly more than their counterparts in the supermarkets.

And these, of course, are not just ordinary wines, they are M&S wines. I wonder sometimes if this theme for an advertising campaign is culturally advisable in straitened Britain, but I am in no doubt that the wines really are special. The whole lot are unique to M&S, and the absence of the universal brands on the shelves does make perusing the range a very much happier experience in this chain than in any other.

Andrew Bird, wine manager at M&S, is quite lofty on the topic of coping with the recession. 'In the current economic climate, a retailer can take one of two routes,' he says. 'Some choose a charge downmarket, throwing quality, provenance and ethical considerations to the wind in the rush to maintain unsustainable prices … And then some stick to their sourcing principles whilst ensuring customers can find true value.' We are left in no doubt which camp M&S belong to.

The wines bear him out. Prices are not up that much, and the best buys include a 10-scoring Gamay costing only £3.99, plus the best-value rosé of the year at the same price. Latin America shines in particular, and I did find several top-of-the-range wines, including a Priorat, that are truly outstanding.

M&S wine departments can be of distinctly varying sizes, and there is no guarantee that all the wines mentioned here will be on sale in every store. But they certainly will be on the website at **www.marksandspencer.com**. A further attraction of the site is that it regularly offers huge discounts on whole-case (6 or 12 bottle) orders, and features numerous wines you cannot buy in the stores. Delivery is usually free if you tick the right box.

Red Wines

 Fragoso Merlot 2008 £5.99
Hearty but not heavy unoaked ripe glugging red, full of life.

9 Altos Condor Malbec 2008 £6.99
Ripe, plummy and smoothly rounded but gripping creamy-oaked blackberry-fruit food wine to go with roast meats. Distinctive example of Argentina's benchmark grape.

 Australian Shiraz 2008 £6.49
From dependable Yalumba winery, a big-hearted pepper and plum, unoaked 14% alcohol, good-value wine.

8 Houghton Cabernet-Shiraz-Merlot 2005 £6.99
Restrained, even elegant, mature Bordeaux-style blend from Australia's oldest winery is structured and satisfying, and 14% alcohol.

8 Pronto 2008 £12.99
The name is catchy, but tells you nothing of this inky-purple, complex grenache-based, old-vine blend from Adelaide; rich black fruit with a toffee background and 14.5% alcohol.

9 Cascabell Monastrell 2007 £15.00
Fantastic slinky-but-grippy Spanish-style oaked red from McLaren Vale (14.5% alcohol) is worth the outlay.

 Soleado Merlot 2008 £4.29
Pleasant, soft, squishy everyday red.

8 Paradiso Carmenère 2008 £5.99
Overtly blackcurrant nose and fruit with a nice grip of the tastebuds, a plump but structured food wine.

RED WINES

9 **Colluvia Syrah 2007** £7.99
Inky-black, assertive, minty, succulent and long-flavoured food wine (roast lamb) with 14.5% alcohol.

8 **Fina Sangre Haras de Pirque 2006** £15.00
Blood colour, rich cassis fruit (it's mostly Cabernet Sauvignon) and seductive smoothness, with 14.5% alcohol, and yet nicely weighted. Drink with expensive beef.

9 **Tobiano San Antonio Pinot Noir 2007** £16.00
This luxury wine is the most likeable Chilean Pinot I've tasted to date: earthy, sweetly edged classic raspberry ripeness in lush, silky texture with 14.5% alcohol.

CHILE

10 **Gamay Vin de Pays d'Ardèche 2008** £3.99
A truly joyful, juicy bargain glugger in the Beaujolais style with focused purple fruit, hint of white pepper and the power to refresh. From the northern Rhône.

8 **Côtes de Gascogne 2008** £4.99
Dense in colour and dark fruit, a healthy, vivid food red.

8 **Premium Fitou 2007** £6.49
Blackberry ripeness in this fleshy but firm southern red.

8 **Mâcon Rouge 2007** £6.99
Easy-drinking, lively strawberry-ripe Pinot to drink cool.

8 **Tentation Richelieu 2005** £7.64
Online only, a modern Merlot-based claret (AC Fronsac) with blackberry and vanilla richness, ripe and ready and 14% alcohol.

FRANCE

RED WINES

9 **Aigle Noir Pinot Noir 2007** £9.99
Attractive limpid ruby colour to this remarkably pure
Pyrenean Pinot, with earthy, summer-pudding fullness.

8 **Rasteau Perrin & Fils 2007** £9.99
Rich and rounded Rhône village wine from top producer
is peppery, long and mature-tasting.

9 **Hermitage Cave de Tain L'Hermitage**
2005 £24.00
From the revered northern Rhône appellation, a fabulous
wine with toasty, gamey aroma, dense colour and rich,
black fruit. Already a pleasure to drink but will develop
over many years. Price is warranted.

FRANCE

8 **Vino da Tavola 2008** £3.99
Simple, juicy and healthy, mainly Sangiovese-Syrah blend
from Italy north and south at a very fair price.

6 **Giardini Red Lower Alcohol 2008** £5.99
Grape-juice-style control-fermented 9.5% alcohol Veneto
Merlot is pleasant enough.

9 **Villa Puccini Toscana 2005** £6.74
Sold only by the case online, this is Chianti – good
Chianti – by another name, bright with red fruits, slinky
and minty, nutty-finishing. Bargain.

9 **Barbera d'Asti Mondo del Vino 2006** £7.49
Classy, sleek and mature rendering of the bouncy-
brambly Barbera style makes a lush, long-flavoured red
to match risotto and pasta (14% alcohol).

ITALY

RED WINES

ITALY

8 La Prendina Estate Corvina 2007 £7.49
From the Valpolicella grape grown in the Valpolicella region, this tastes very like ... you guessed it! Healthy, sweetly ripe, keenly refreshing.

8 Barbaresco Umberto Fiore 2005 £9.99
You don't often see this exotic name from Piedmont on the shelf, and this is a good one, already browning in colour with a spirity, rose-petal nose and authentic sweet-but-spare red fruit. Rare find under £10.

9 Renato Ratti Nebbiolo 2007 £10.99
I have an uncorrectable weakness for this Piedmont perennial. It may be the riverbank name, but more likely the deep ruby colour, lush-but-tannin-rimmed sleek red fruit and surprising intensity (14% alcohol).

SOUTH AFRICA

9 Maara Shiraz 2008 £5.99
Characteristically roasted aroma of this bold Fairtrade red reveals an elegant, gently spicy fruit. Silky and superior.

8 Houdamond Pinotage 2007 £8.99
Bumper indigenous red has lush, creamy style but a brisk, bright fruitiness; 14% alcohol but nicely poised.

8 Journey's End Beefwood Cabernet 2005 £9.89
Online only, a generous but restrained Cape 'claret' with toasty oak overtones. Lovely.

RED WINES

SPAIN

10 **Les Mines Bellmunt del Priorat 2006** **£12.99**
Priorat is a cult region in Spain, and this monster (15% alcohol) substantiates its status with its black depths, elderberry whiff and gamey-leather-savoury nuances. Thoroughly Spanish, and rarely affordable by Priorat standards.

USA

8 **Teichert Ranch Petite Sirah 2007** **£7.99**
Dense, inky colour and crème de cassis nose but a nicely weighted, dry-finishing black-fruit Californian.

PINK WINES

CHILE

8 **Montgras Zinfandel Rosé 2009** **£6.49**
Pale smoked-salmon colour to this pleasingly fresh and healthy dry strawberry-ripe wine. It has depth, and would be a good food wine – with just about anything.

FRANCE

7 **Rosé d'Anjou 2008** **£5.49**
Old-fashioned faintly sweet Loire pink has redeeming strawberry freshness.

ITALY

7 **Vinicola Talamonti Montepulciano Rosé** **£6.99**
This is pink Montepulciano d'Abruzzo and tastes like it – strong, near-red colour, vigorous brambly fruit with a hint of sweetness. Quite fun.

SPAIN

9 **Las Falleras Rosé 2008** **£3.99**
Magenta coloured from Utiel-Requena, this dry wine has soft-fruit flavours; it really does taste pink, has a mild 11.5% alcohol, and is cheap. All the true virtues of rosé!

PINK WINES

SPAIN

🍷7 **Moscatel Rosado 2008** £5.49
Magenta stickie from Valencia has honeyed, grapey sweeness and just 10% alcohol. A fun aperitif to drink very cold.

WHITE WINES

AUSTRALIA

🍷8 **Australian Chardonnay 2008** £6.49
Made by Yalumba, a nice greeny-gold colour and generous plump melon fruit with crisp finish. Stands out.

🍷8 **Tasmanian Sauvignon Blanc 2008** £7.99
Nice tingly, asparagus-scented Sauvignon with weight and freshness in equal abundance. Good food matcher.

CHILE

🍷8 **Soleado Sauvignon Blanc 2008** £4.29
Brisk and satisfyingly intense green-fruit party wine.

🍷8 **Tierra y Hombre Sauvignon Blanc 2008** £5.49
Impressive ripe gooseberry-fresh wine with nettly zest.

FRANCE

🍷8 **Le Froglet Chardonnay 2008** £4.99
Don't let the iffy name put you off this pleasantly clean, oaked Mediterranean vin de pays.

🍷7 **VPVL Sauvignon Blanc 2008** £4.99
Straight, brisk Loire refresher at a fair price.

🍷8 **Alsace Pinot Blanc 2008** £6.99
From ubiquitous Cave de Turckheim, a melon-ripe but mineral-fresh example of the now-elusive Pinot Blanc.

WHITE WINES

8 **Sauvignon Blanc de St Bris 2008** £7.99
Made by famed co-op La Chablisienne, this rare burgundy Sauvignon has a flinty character akin to Chablis and eager citrus highlights.

9 **Bourgogne Chardonnay 2007** £8.99
This is terrific; ideal mélange of sweet-apple fruit, toasty mellowness and bright acidity, it convincingly evokes its place of origin: Meursault.

9 **Chablis La Chablisienne 2007** £9.99
Just a humble Chablis AC (not a '1er cru') but a really inspiring flinty-creamy classic wine of a region ill-represented in supermarkets.

8 **Collioure Blanc Cave de l'Abbé Rous 2007** £9.99
Pyrenean curiosity is a luxury rich-but-edgy, toasty and near-unctuous dry white to match shellfish and saucy seafood (14% alcohol).

FRANCE

10 **Palataia Pinot Grigio 2008** £6.99
Smoky, intense and remarkably long-flavoured Rheinpfalz dry wine exploits the popularity of Italian Pinot Grigio, and upstages it for quality and value. Best PG of the year.

9 **Darting Estate Weissburgunder Eiswein**
2007 37.5cl £14.99
Great rarity from the Rheinpfalz is golden, ambrosial, beautifully balanced and 9% alcohol. Treat as an aperitif rather than a dessert wine.

GERMANY

WHITE WINES

ITALY

🍷 8 **Beneventano Bianco 2008** £4.29
M&S's Italian house white from Benevento, north-east of
Naples, is a perennial bargain. Orchard-blossom aromas,
dry but subtly peachy fruit, fresh and friendly.

🍷 8 **Quatro Sei Gavi 2008** £6.49
Aroma of blossom and brassica, exotic dry fruit, almond
richness; distinctive food wine (fish or creamy pastas)
with just 11.5% alcohol.

🍷 8 **Pecorino Contesa 2007** £9.99
Rich colour to this exotic Abruzzo food wine (with
cheese, including unrelated Pecorino if you like) is echoed
in this complex but crisp, dry white.

NEW ZEALAND

🍷 9 **Kaituna Hills Blue 2008** £5.99
Sauvignon/Semillon blend has asparagus whiff and
grassy-tropical-fruit counterpoint. Very Kiwi, great
value.

🍷 8 **Seifried Nelson Sauvignon Blanc 2008** £7.99
What particularly stands out in this workmanlike nettly-
fresh wine is the background sweet ripeness, which will
suit those who don't like their Sauvignon too green.

🍷 8 **Kaituna Hills Pinot Grigio 2008** £9.99
Spookily like a superior Alsace Pinot Gris, this has exotic
gently spiced tropical fruit but finishes dry with a nice
lemon twist.

WHITE WINES

SOUTH AFRICA

8 **Maara Chardonnay 2008** £5.99
Lots of ripe apple-pie flavour for the money. A Fairtrade wine.

8 **Workhouse Ken Forrester Chenin Blanc 2008** £6.99
Zingy top flavour to this lush, long and refreshing food wine (rich fish recipes and white meats).

SPAIN

7 **Spanish Macabeo 2008** £3.99
Simple brassica-scented clean dry white at a keen price.

9 **Cuatro Rayas Rueda Verdejo 2008** £5.99
Impactful green first flavour and lush long brassica-peach combo in flavour gives this length and dimension. Good food wine – mackerel, tapas.

8 **Val do Salnes Albariño 2007** £9.99
Such a big flavour in this long, vegetal, grassy-fresh Galician dry wine. Needs food – even gazpacho.

USA

8 **Schug Carneros Chardonnay 2007** £16.00
Extravagant oaked Sonoma wine is straw colour, lavishly peachy and ripe. Sinfully delicious and strictly for special occasions.

FORTIFIED WINES

PORTUGAL

7 **Extra Dry White Port 50cl** £7.99
Very pale, very dry wine with only a passing resemblance to port. Nice grippy aperitif, though (19% alcohol).

6 **Pink Port** £7.99
Magenta curiosity has had much hype but to me tastes like some sort of bumped-up Douro table wine.

FORTIFIED WINES

SPAIN

9 Manzanilla £5.99
By dependable Williams & Humbert, a smoky-salty-tangy sherry of transcending crispness and freshness (15% alcohol). A real find.

SPARKLING WINES

ENGLAND

7 English Sparkling Brut £16.99
Well-coloured, florally perfumed, generously fruity fizz doesn't ape champagne but has much merit.

FRANCE

9 Champagne Oudinot Brut £19.99
Very consistent house champagne has nice brioche whiff and long, developed flavours. Often on discount but a safe bet at list price anyway.

8 Champagne Louis Chaurey Brut £25.99
A new one to me, rich in colour, intense, long and even sumptuous fruit. Nice surprise.

**9 Champagne Saint Gall Grand Cru
Brut 2002** £26.99
Fab vintage champagne at a fair price is de luxe all the way, with rich gold colour, creamy mousse, lots of appley-creamy Chardonnay fruit. Plush!

ITALY

8 Sparkling Pinot Noir 2007 £7.99
Brightly pink Piedmont fizz has recognisable strawberry Pinot flavours and an endearing freshness.

N ZEALAND

8 Bluff Hills Blanc de Blancs 2006 £9.99
Gold colour to this soft, creamy, foaming Gisborne Chardonnay (11.5% alcohol), finishing very crisp.

─── *Morrisons* ───

Ho hum. I have not been invited to taste the Morrisons wine range in 2009, and cruising the wine department in my local megastore leads me to believe that this part of the business is not a priority at present. So just a very few recommendations in this truncated section.

RED WINES

AUSTRALIA

🍷7 **Roo Brothers Shiraz 2007** £5.99
Lightish in colour but a really firm, briary and attention-grabbing red with 14% alcohol.

🍷8 **Tyrells Heathcote Shiraz 2006** £8.22
Swish silky-spicy Hunter Valley is deliciously savoury and will develop for years in bottle; 14.5% alcohol.

FRANCE

🍷8 **Les Jamelles Cabernet Sauvignon 2008** £5.29
Successful Languedoc brand has concentrated blackberry fruit and healthy grip of tannin. Convincing.

🍷8 **Grande Réserve Corbières 2003** £8.29
If there's any of this left, pounce: a robust and brambly Languedoc full of ripeness and years, smoothed by oak-ageing.

🍷8 **Château Caronne Ste Gemme 1999** £9.99
This perpetual Médoc from a decent and now-mature vintage is worth seeking out: firm blackcurrant fruit, grippy and long.

ITALY

🍷9 **Morrisons The Best Montepulciano 2003** £5.49
Unusual to find this wine with any bottle age but if you find it, a real treat: juicy but smoothly rounded.

WHITE WINES

AUSTRALIA

8 **Cookoothama Botrytis**
Semillon 2005 37.5cl £11.99
Honeyed 'dessert' wine better as an aperitif is
astonishingly rich and exotic, with notions of peach,
pineapple and mango. Equal to a good Sauternes in
interest (and, sadly, in price).

FRANCE

8 **La Différence Viognier Muscat 2008** £4.99
A dry white from the Languedoc but with grapy, mellow,
almondy flavours from the enticing Viognier-Muscat
blend.

8 **Sichel Sauternes 2005** £9.29
As good as much pricier château-made Sauternes, this is
sumptuously rich in colour and fruit and with a trim
acidity. Gorgeous.

8 **Meursault Le Meurger 2006** £14.99
I bought this in a fit of madness and was immensely
relieved when it turned out rich, peachy-creamy and
balanced.

N ZEALAND

9 **Seifried Sauvignon Blanc 2008** £8.20
One of my favourite Kiwi Sauvignons, bristling with
aromas of nettles and gooseberries and alive with grassy
fruit.

SPAIN

8 **Torres Viña Sol 2008** £5.99
Lively and refreshing big-brand from Barcelona region
gushes with orchard fruit and refreshment.

Sainsbury's

The star turn among Sainsbury's wines continues to be the Taste the Difference range, launched in 2006 and now an institution. The quality and distinctiveness of these wines, extending from Bordeaux to the other classic regions of France, across most of the Continent and into the New World, are consistent, and often outstanding. Prices are sensible.

I like the 1.5-litre ribbed-plastic bottles of French plonk that have been introduced in honour of the recession. It's a nice bit of austerity nostalgia after the vulgarity of the 'record period of sustained growth' that was the boom of the past decade, and the wines are really not bad.

And I also like Sainsbury's idea of a 'style guide' for their own-label wines, colour-coding each of them into one of six categories. Examples are whites deemed 'crisp and delicate' or conversely 'complex and elegant', and reds that are either 'smooth and mellow' or 'rich and complex'. The idea is that customers who like this or that style can then simply seek out the right colour coding when they wish to try something different – but not too different.

The new labels also offer food-matching recommendations. I was interested to see that a great many of the more robust red wines bore the suggestion that 'roast red meats, game and cheese' were the right partners. But I wonder if roast red meats and game are really such regular items on the menu of very many households these days. And cheese is a notoriously clashy match for big red wines.

But this is carping. Sainsbury's intend to be of service to their customers, and you cannot fault that. There are lots of good wines, perhaps not as many as I remember in previous years, but a new wine manager in 2009, Justin James, is reassuring: 'My aim is to make our range attractive to our customers, comprising a good balance of must-stock brands with increasing opportunities to discover more interesting own-label wines to trade up and try.'

RED WINES

ARGENTINA

♥ 10 Taste the Difference Malbec 2007   £5.99
Brilliant balance of Malbec's 'leather and spice' chewiness and mellow ripeness makes this 14.5% alcohol smoothie an exceptional buy.

♥ 8 Sainsbury's Australian Merlot   £3.69
Plump but not soggy mouthfiller delivers much for the money.

**♥ 9 Hardy's Oomoo Grenache-Shiraz-
          Mourvedre 2006**   £7.19
Rich and dark with caramel richness and 14% alcohol, this Hardy's special is irresistibly artful, seductive and long. It's not just the herd of emus on the label.

AUSTRALIA

♥ 9 Willunga 100 Grenache 2007   £7.99
Rich chocolatey McLaren Vale monster (14.5% alcohol) has delicately poised, cushy weightiness. Nice tree-motif label.

♥ 8 Limited Release McLaren Vale Shiraz 2008 £8.99
Black in colour and fruit but with lush, yielding and gently spicy highlights and texture, and 14.5% alcohol.

♥ 10 Gulf Station Pinot Noir 2008   £9.99
A really focused and vivid essence-of-soft-fruit Pinot from Yarra Valley's De Bortoli winery. It is pure magic, and a true challenge to the supremacy of Burgundy.

CHILE

♥ 7 Sainsbury's Chilean Merlot 2008   £3.31
Wholesome party red is value for money.

RED WINES

CHILE

9 **Taste the Difference Chilean Merlot 2007**   £5.99
This really stands out for silky purity of flavour and well-judged weight. Textbook oaking, supple texture; lovely plummy style with 14% alcohol.

8 **Merlot Vin de Pays de la Cité de**
Carcassonne 2008   £3.99
Sweet black-cherry centre to this firmly flavoured food matcher – try chicken or charcuterie.

9 **Sainsbury's Beaujolais**   £3.99
Eager, vivid blend-of-vintages Beaujolais captures the magic of this unique style; a bargain to drink cool.

8 **Sainsbury's Cuvée Prestige**
Côtes du Rhône 2008   £4.79
Dense crimson with eager black fruit, a pinch of pepper and 14% alcohol.

FRANCE

8 **Chinon Domaine du Colombier 2007**   £5.99
Distinctive Loire red has typical pale colour, leafy-stalky aroma and nicely abrading raspberry fruit.

9 **Taste the Difference Côtes du Rhône**
Villages 2007   £5.99
Robust and intense blackberry and spice oaked heavyweight (14.5% alcohol) by ace producer Max Chapoutier. Good value.

8 **Sainsbury's Vin Rouge de France 1.5L**   £6.67
In a two-bottle-size ribbed plastic container, a recession-busting, purple, brambly glugger evoking what the label claims is 'ripe raspberries and cherries'. I loved it!

RED WINES

**8 Sainsbury's Cabernet Sauvignon
Vin de Pays d'Oc 1.5L** £6.79
Packaged as the preceding Vin Rouge, a gripping but not
fierce blackcurranty picnic wine with backbone.

7 Duboeuf Brouilly 2007 £7.49
A juicy and crisp Beaujolais cru to drink with food; above
average for quality, at a price.

8 Crozes Hermitage Cave de Tain 2006 £7.99
Very ripe, near-raisiny all-Syrah northern Rhône is
roundly mature with long spicy flavours.

8 Taste the Difference St Emilion 2007 £8.99
From reliable Dourthe company, a plump, toasty claret
more New World in style than elegant St Emilion, but
very, very likeable.

8 Château de la Garde 2006 £9.49
Poised, mature right-bank claret has ripe black fruit,
creamy oak and velvet-grip tannins.

8 Sainsbury's Valpolicella £3.42
Pale, not thin, cherry-fruit lightweight (11.5% alcohol)
has pleasing nutty-dry finish and alluring price.

8 Canti Merlot Sangiovese 2008 £4.39
Big brand but a fetchingly plump and juicy Sicilian at a
good price.

9 Sainsbury's Chianti 2008 £4.65
Cracking Chianti with keen cherry-blackberry fruit, long
flavours and brisk nutty finish. Real bargain.

FRANCE

ITALY

Red Wines

Sainsbury's

7 Casa Mia Sangiovese 2008   £5.99
Deep-maroon Sicilian summer-fruit wine from the grape
of Chianti.

**8 Vino Nobile di Montepulciano
San Colombaio 2005**   £10.99
Browning mature almost spirity minty monster with
coffee and cinnamon notes in its dark, endless depths.
Lovely stuff.

8 Taste the Difference Amarone 2006   £14.59
A top-end example of this quirky spin on Valpolicella,
coal-dark in colour and even flavour with sweet centre
and 'bitter' (amarone) finish; 14.5% alcohol.

**9 Taste the Difference Marlborough
Pinot Noir 2008**   £8.99
Pale but not wan, a shamelessly commercial strawberry-
ripe and lively aperitif of great charm to drink cool.

8 Tinto da Anfora 2006   £5.99
From Alentejo, a porty, vanilla-rich, vigorously fruity
dark food wine with minty, silky appeal and 14% alcohol.

8 Sainsbury's Fairtrade Pinotage 2007   £4.99
Lighter than expected (though 14% alcohol) I liked the
gamey-spicy, authentic style; good with chili dishes.

ITALY

N ZEALAND

PORTUGAL

SOUTH AFRICA

RED WINES

8 **SO Organic South African Cabernet Sauvignon 2008** £4.99

SOUTH AFRICA

Also a Fairtrade wine, it's big, blackcurranty, ripe (14% alcohol) and clean-edged; ignore back-label suggestion to drink it with cheese: the tannins would make the two clash like cymbals.

8 **Solagüen Rioja Gran Reserva 1999** £15.99

SPAIN

Oloroso colour, pruny nose and sumptuous summer-pudding fruit in this fabulous and fabulously expensive classic.

PINK WINES

8 **Sainsbury's Chilean Rosé 2008** £3.99

CHILE

Salmon colour, and juicy blackcurrant flavour true to the Cabernet Sauvignon it's made from; dry and satisfying.

7 **Domaine de Sours Rosé 2008** £5.99

FRANCE

Magenta Bordeaux strays to the sweet side, but is correctly clean at the finish. Will suit sweeter tastes.

7 **Sainsbury's Portuguese Rosé** £3.02

PORTUGAL

Salmon colour, floral smell, confected but not cloying fruit, 10% alcohol and very cheap.

WHITE WINES

AUSTRALIA

8 **Sainsbury's Australian Chardonnay** £3.75
Oaked, toffeeish but pleasingly fresh, a very decent non-vintage party wine at an amazing price.

8 **Leasingham Magnus Riesling 2007** £7.99
Lush, limey and long food wine will do justice to barbecued poultry and shellfish.

8 **Taste the Difference Adelaide Hills**
Chardonnay 2007 £7.99
Yellow, apple-pie-rich and long-flavoured with trim acidity and 14% alcohol.

8 **Taste the Difference Grüner Veltliner 2008** £6.99
Rich colour, sunny fruit salad flavours with hill herbs, lemon finish; unique dry wine of real charm.

CHILE

7 **Cono Sur Gewürztraminer 2008** £5.99
Hallmark lychee aroma and likeable tropical fruit.

8 **Taste the Difference Chilean**
Sauvignon Blanc 2008 £5.99
Artfully made refresher has leafy, asparagus-like greeness in counterpoint to a slyly delicious sweetness. Very appealing.

FRANCE

8 **Jacques Lurton Sauvignon Blanc 2008** £4.99
Loire refresher is gooseberry bright and an ideal mussels match.

8 **Taste the Difference Muscadet**
Sèvre et Maine Sur Lie 2008 £5.99
Good extracted smell, briny, bracing but generous fruit. Good example of the famed Loire seafood wine.

WHITE WINES

9 **Taste the Difference Vouvray 2008** £6.96
Autumn-ripe, honey-hinting, just-dry Loire aperitif is sinfully lush; tastes very expensive.

9 **Taste the Difference Gewürztraminer 2007** £7.29
A noticeable step up from the usual supermarket Alsace Gewürz from the Turckheim co-operative, this has a huge lychee aroma, long tropical-spicy flavours and a defining limey acidity.

9 **Chablis La Chablisienne 2007** £8.99
Well-coloured, immediately recognisable flinty but friendly, seductive Chablis.

9 **Taste the Difference Pouilly Fumé 2008** £10.98
Vintage after vintage, this Loire classic is persistently brilliant. Lovely pointy Sauvignon with shimmering complexity and minerality.

8 **Sancerre La Moussière 2008** £14.99
Worthy of the name and made by top-rated Mellot family, a fine, flinty and expensive Loire high-flyer.

9 **Dr L Riesling 2008** £6.79
Racy but generous apple-perfumed stony-fresh Moselle has masses of pure fruit and only 8.5% alcohol.

8 **Sainsbury's Hungarian Pinot Grigio 2008** £3.99
A good tilt at the enduring PG craze, grassy-fresh, a bit of green spice, nice citrus edge.

WHITE WINES

ITALY

7 **Sainsbury's Frascati Superiore 2008** £3.97
Brisk grassy style to this Roman favourite at a fair price.

7 **Sainsbury's Soave Colli Scaligieri 2008** £3.99
'Crisp and delicate' says the chatty label but it's really quite sweet – insinuating, though, as an aperitif.

8 **Sainsbury's Pinot Grigio delle Venezie 2008** £4.49
Made by industrial-scale producer Cavit, but this has a fetching green twang at the edge. PG with more life than many.

8 **Casa Mia Fiano 2008** £5.99
Sicilian favourite has mellow, herbaceous flavours.

8 **Rocca Vecchia Pinot Grigio 2008** £9.99
If you're up for spending a tenner on PG, get this one, a properly aromatic mountain wine with tangy, smoky flavours, long fruit and exotic character. Food wine – try smoked fish or meat.

NEW ZEALAND

7 **Sanctuary Sauvignon Blanc 2008** £6.99
Straight Marlborough wine, leafy aroma, grassy lushness.

8 **Sacred Hill Marlborough
Sauvignon Blanc 2008** £8.99
Masses of interest in this well-built mélange of flavours all in a zingy, lingering package. Worth paying the extra.

SPARKLING WINES

9 Sainsbury's Blanc de Noirs Brut £15.99
Consistently pleasing, full-flavoured, toasty-nosed house
champagne.

8 Sainsbury's Rosé Champagne £18.99
Attractive coral colour, crisp, strawberry fruit, a genuine
refresher.

9 Taste the Difference Champagne 2003 £19.99
Mellowness and depth are welcome features of this
vintage champagne at non-vintage price.

7 Sainsbury's Sparkling Pinot Grigio £6.49
A cynical contrivance, but not as bad as it sounds: breezy,
smoky fruit, good persistent mousse.

7 Sainsbury's Cava Brut £4.38
Edgy, orchard-fruit-busy sparkler will make a good mixer
for Bellinis. I preferred it to its vintage counterpart,
priced at £11.99.

Tesco

Tesco has been doing some research. 'Customers are telling us they have less money and less time,' reports wine department manager Andrew Carpenter. 'So we have to ensure that we have the right range of products in the right place and at the right price to make customers' lives as easy as possible.'

You'd better believe it. The legend in the trade is that Tesco sells a quarter of all the wine we drink at home in Britain, and this giant is not about to give up any of that lion's share. The wines get better and better, the prices are maintained – at what cost to suppliers I dread to think – and there are always bargains to be had.

This is especially true on the internet (**www.tesco.com**), where the full range of more than a thousand wines is on offer for home delivery, along with lots of online-only wines, many of them 'parcels' from producers far too small to distribute among the branches, but of real interest. If you join the Tesco Wine Club, you get regular updates and offers, both in the post and online.

Tesco outlets range from corner-shop size to monstrous megastores, so they stock very variable wine ranges. If any of the wines recommended here are missing, look online or phone the order line 08456 775577.

RED WINES

8 **Peter Lehmann The Clancy 2005** £7.53
Bold, peppery and slurpily fruity Cabernet-Shiraz-Merlot blend at 14.5% alcohol to match with a robust pie; even has a hint of Daddies Sauce.

8 **Finest Howcroft Estate Cabernet Merlot 2006** £7.99
Subtly balanced and oaked smoothie made by a lady called Helen Foggo.

8 **Ringbolt Margaret River Cabernet Sauvignon 2007** £8.39
Flavour evokes new-picked blackberries. Intense (14.5% alcohol) and tannic but fresh and vivid. Try with pasta or anything meaty.

9 **Finest Yarra Valley Pinot Noir 2007** £13.49
Gorgeous earthy Pinot nose on this pale but jumpingly juicy rustic-raspberry classic from legendary De Bortoli winery. Pricy except when compared to inferior village burgundies.

9 **The Feathered Dinosaur Cabernet Sauvignon 2004** £18.99
From the great d'Arenberg winery in McLaren Vale, this is about the same colour as Guinness, an elecric soup of savoury enormity, 14.5% alcohol and unforgettable fruit.

7 **Tesco Chilean Cabernet Sauvignon 2008** £3.07
Short, muscular and darkly concentrated chili-matcher. Very cheap.

RED WINES

CHILE

7 **Tesco Chilean Merlot 2008**   £3.27
Made by respectable Cono Sur, a brightly purple glugger
with coffee notes, brambly sweetness, even a whiff of
spice – and cheap.

8 **Cono Sur Pinot Noir 2008**   £6.09
Astoundingly consistent well-mulched cherry-fruit
perennial is grippingly good in this new vintage, with
14% alcohol.

8 **Vieille Fontaine 2008**   £3.29
Vin de pays d'Oc from Plaimont co-op has a big
raspberry nose, fleshy ripeness and juicy top flavour.

9 **Tesco Claret**   £3.38
Fellow tasters on the day scorned this non-vintage wine
but I was taken in by its soft, mature charm and Bordeaux
balance almost as much as by the amazing price.

FRANCE

7 **Mont Tauch Winegrowers
Reserve Fitou 2007**   £5.99
Eye-catching radical label on this brisk, spicy Languedoc
red from famed Fitou co-operative.

7 **Finest Médoc 2007**   £6.83
Still a bit green but lots of plummy, eager fruit and grip.
Keep till Christmas 2010.

8 **Arrogant Frog Rural Red 2007**   £6.99
Never mind the puerile branding, this is a dark, dense
and vigorous vin de pays d'Oc with a stimulating briary
nose and gently gripping black fruit. 'Leaps out of the
glass with New World attitude,' says Tesco. Ho ho.

RED WINES

9 **Domaine de la Grande Bellane**
Côtes du Rhône Villages 2007 £6.99
Proper monster (14.5% alcohol) of opaque colour and matching density of spicy-leafy-liquorous black fruit. Classic of its kind, keenly priced. Will keep.

8 **St Chinian Roches Noires 2006** £7.99
Gamey-spicy, quite fiercely brambly fruit bomb from excellent Cave de Roquebrun is just the right side of jammy and will mellow with the years.

10 **Finest St Emilion 2007** £8.98
Cunningly contrived new-era claret of epic weight and concentration with toffee hints of new-oak ageing is also elegant and poised, alive with vivid fruit. Fabulous.

9 **Château Reysson 2005** £9.99
Stalwart Haut-Médoc 'Cru Bourgeois Supérieur' in a great vintage is robustly ripe and intense with proper cedar-plummy claret character. Unusually good value.

7 **Château Tronquoy Lalande 2003** £13.69
Famed chateau of St Estèphe is still darkly purple despite age, but full of promise. Keep till 2013.

7 **Mercurey Clos La Marche**
Louis Max 2006 £14.99
Pale, elusive burgundy (Chalonnais) has eager red-fruit Pinot nose and silky, unfolding flavours. Special occasions only.

FRANCE

RED WINES

FRANCE

🍷8 **Les Tourelles de Longueville 2006**   £22.99
'Second' wine of famed grand cru classé is a fraction of the price of the grand vin itself. Classic claret of unforgettable purity and plushness you can drink now or keep.

🍷8 **Nuits St Georges Domaine de Perdrix 2001**   £27.99
We can all dream, can't we? Lovely slinky burgundy in fat maturity with lots of colour and toasty fruits. Buy this one, not the 2000 at the same price.

ITALY

🍷10 **Siciliano Rosso 2008**   £3.23
Fantastic glugging island red brings sweet-herbaceous character to redcurrant and cherry fruit. Lovely easy weight, refreshing served cool, comforting with pasta dishes. Unbelievably cheap.

🍷8 **Finest Nero d'Avola 2008**   £5.99
Syrupy nose of this purple Sicilian gives way to long, squishy-but-grippy dry-finishing roasted fruit. Delish!

🍷10 **Finest Valpolicella Ripasso 2006**   £6.14
Made by Girelli, the people behind the Canaletto brand, this is outstanding – cushion-soft and yet nuttily edgy texture to a dark, rich fruit. Bargain.

🍷9 **Finest Barbera D'Asti Fratelli Martini 2005** £6.99
Juicy-sweet Piedmont bouncer has ideal pasta-matching weight and nutty finish. Look out for this wine at occasional promo price of about a fiver.

RED WINES

**8 Inycon Limited Edition
Cabernet Sauvignon 2007**   £8.99

Sicilian blockbuster has the trademark island hill-herb nuances over powerful Cabernet black-fruit flavours.

7 Ogio Primitivo 2007   £8.99

Rugged, hearty Puglian red with darkly spicy depths is forever on promo at half price, which promotes its score from 7 to 9.

9 Masi Campofiorin 2006   £9.99

Veronese curio is really a supercharged Valpolicella, gutsy, velvety and yet keenly edgy with red fruit flavours. Gorgeous, distinctive wine.

**8 Rocca Alata Amarone Della
Valpolicella 2006**   £14.63

Dense speciality red has a macaroon richness topped by a bitter-chocolate dryness. It's a sort of after-dinner port substitute and 14.5% alcohol. Good of its kind.

8 Finest Barolo Ascheri Giacomo 2005   £14.99

Lovely translucent ruby colour to this unusually substantial example of Italy's most overrated red wine.

8 Chateau Musar 2001   £14.99

Famed wine of wartorn Bekaa Valley is quite pale and brown but holding up nicely with spice and grippy preserved fruit and underlying sweet ripeness. An endearing curio.

ITALY

LEBANON

RED WINES

NEW ZEALAND

♥9 **The Reach Merlot 2007** £6.99
Pure-fruit, silky, typically Kiwi plump-black-cherry style
from Hawkes Bay.

♥8 **Babich Gimblett Gravels Syrah 2006** £8.21
Very Kiwi spin on the grape of the northern Rhône, this
is a cool, minty, silky red something like a St Joseph.
Convincing.

♥8 **Finest Marlborough Pinot Noir 2007** £8.99
Artful, lush, eucalypt-style is good value by Kiwi
standards.

SOUTH AFRICA

♥7 **Tesco South African Red** £3.24
Strangely appealing burnt-rubber smell and tarry
background to this easy-drinking Cape non-vintage
plonk.

♥9 **Beyers Truter Pinotage 2007** £8.19
Roast-chestnut and cinnamon seem stirred into this lush,
plummy winter red. Very South African (and 14.5%
alcohol) and very delicious with meaty dishes.

♥8 **Flagstone Dragon Tree 2006** £10.19
Slick, ripe, opulent multi-grape blend with recognisable
roasted Cape perfume but genuinely elegant weight and
structure. Serious stuff (14% alcohol) justifying the
awkward price.

♥9 **Kanonkop Paul Sauer 2005** £17.99
Famed Stellenbosch name is, in effect, Cape claret, but
with a maturity, ripeness and power (14.5% alcohol) all
its own. Fabulous.

RED WINES

SPAIN

8 **Gran Tesoro Garnacha 2008** £3.49
From just south of Rioja, a lively, spicy young red to scoff with fiery foods. Fresh but not green.

9 **Cano Cosecha Toro 2007** £5.19
Luminous crimson colour and long flavours in this roasty, blackcurranty wine. Great value.

8 **Cosme Palacio Rioja 2006** £8.99
Modern undesignated Rioja has obvious vanilla-oak influence but good, silky fruit in equal abundance. Better, if not cheaper, than other popular brands.

8 **Baron de Ley Finca Monastario 2006** £16.02
De luxe Rioja is opaque, hugely ripe (14% alcohol) and rich with creamy cassis fruit. Tastes as expensive as it is.

PINK WINES

AUSTRALIA

8 **Tesco Chardonnay Rosé 2008** £4.49
Pink shardy! Magenta colour comes from just 5% red wine and the gentle toffee notes from the sweet Chardonnay fruit.

N ZEALAND

7 **The Reach Sauvignon Blanc Rosé 2008** £7.99
Onion-skin colour, sweet cherry nose, off-dry; colour is from added Pinot Noir.

PINK WINES

SPAIN

🍷7 **Gran Tesoro Garnacha Rosé 2008** £3.49
Shocking pink, brambly-briary dryness over sweet, jammy fruit.

🍷9 **Finest Navarra Garnacha Rosé 2008** £6.14
Magenta wine has crunch, juiciness and briskness, and tastes positively pink.

🍷7 **Torres Viña Sol Rosé 2008** £6.49
Shocking pink, Ribena-style, pleasantly dry.

WHITE WINES

ARGENTINA

🍷7 **Finest Guentota Chardonnay Viognier 2008** £7.99
Hefty unoaked food wine (fishcakes, chicken) with long, peachy tail.

AUSTRALIA

🍷8 **Big Kahuna White** £4.99
Brassica nose followed up by conventional oaked Oz Chardonnay style is satisfying and good value.

🍷9 **Finest Tingleup Great Southern
Riesling 2008** £6.99
Proper dry, limey Oz Riesling with mineral defintion and generous concentration. Top food wine – fish, fowl, rice.

🍷8 **Finest Block 7a Viognier 2007** £7.19
Honey background but an emphatically dry style to this ripe, concentrated rendition from the Murray Darling.

🍷8 **Finest Denman Vineyard Chardonnay 2007** £7.99
Extravagant yellow colour – and flavours – in this custardy but crisply edged Hunter Valley classic.

White Wines

AUSTRALIA

8 **Finest Kenton Valley Vineyard
Sauvignon Blanc 2007**   £7.99
Beach grass comes to mind when you sniff this breezy
Adelaide refresher; long, intense matching flavours. For
surfers, not for wimps.

8 **Tim Adams Semillon 2006**   £9.22
Distinctive tropical style to this Clare Valley classic with
a comforting twinning of pineapple lushness and grassy
zest. The most perfect white wine to drink with roast
chicken.

CHILE

9 **Finest Los Nogales Sauvignon Blanc 2008**   £7.54
Terrific nettly nose from this heralded the liveliest
Sauvignon of the day; shimmering lush-grass flavours,
lovely limey finish.

FRANCE

9 **Vieille Fontaine 2008**   £3.29
Tangy Sauvignon-style vin de pays d'Oc with lifted
lemony acidity. Light touch with 11.5% alcohol.

9 **Tesco Mâcon Villages 2008**   £5.48
Standout bargain burgundy has yellow colour, toffee-
apple nose, light but firm classic mineral Chardonnay
fruit. Brill.

7 **Premiere Anjou Blanc 2007**   £5.69
Here's one out of the box, a dry Chenin Blanc, full of
brisk fruit, from an appellation known only for rosé.
Brave but not cheap.

WHITE WINES

FRANCE

9 **Tesco White Burgundy 2007** £5.98
Lots of lemon-gold colour in this convincing apple-pie Maconnais; pure unoaked Chardonnay of great character. Cheap.

8 **Gerard Bertrand Dry Muscat 2008** £5.99
Smells Muscatty, but is indeed dry (with a honey trace) on the palate, and eagerly fresh.

8 **Les Montgolfiers Sauvignon Blanc
Gros Manseng 2008** £6.99
Gascon vin de pays has plush fruit-salad style; match with shellfish.

8 **Laurent Miquel Nord Sud Viognier 2007** £7.99
Big, fat vin de pays d'Oc is almost oily in its richness, yet nicely trimmed with acidity. Artful.

ITALY

9 **Finest Fiano 2008** £5.99
Lovable Sicilian is richly coloured, florally perfumed, distinctively exotic and both lush and tangy.

8 **Alta Italia Pinot Grigio Valdadige 2008** £6.99
Nice wood-smoke whiff from this tangy, super-fresh sub-Alpine PG to serve with creamy pastas or seafood.

7 **Dino Pinot Grigio 2008** £7.99
Look out for this decent crisp PG on regular half-price discount.

WHITE WINES

NEW ZEALAND

8 **Fern Bay Sauvignon Blanc 2008**　　　£4.99
Crisp-finishing over a lot of sweetly ripe fruit (but only 11.5% alcohol), this is as cheap as good Kiwi Sauvignon gets, and not bad.

8 **Finest Autumn-Picked Riesling 2008**　　£7.99
Marlborough wine so like Moselle (even has trademark 8.5% alcohol) that it challenges German exclusivity. Sunny apple-juice style.

8 **The Reach Sauvignon Blanc 2008**　　　£8.19
Mouthful of gooseberries with nettle zing and grassy tail – the full Sauvignon experience. Assertive Marlborough food wine to go with fish, rice, Asian.

PORTUGAL

7 **Tagus Creek Chardonnay Fernao Pires 2008**　　　£5.49
Interesting slaking dry wine to match oily fish.

SOUTH AFRICA

9 **Vergelegen Sauvignon Blanc 2008**　　　£8.01
Great name, great wine, fair price for a lavish, concentratedly lush and long, stony-fresh special-occasion bottle.

8 **Neil Ellis Stellenbosch Chardonnay 2007**　　£9.19
Cabbage nose, sweet-apple fruit in this weighty (14% alcohol) oaked luxury wine.

WHITE WINES

SPAIN

🍷10 **Gran Tesoro Viura 2008** £3.49
Very pale, but with an appreciable lemon/asparagus nose,
this delivers a positive whack of ripe, generous grassy-
lush fruit. Amazing value.

🍷7 **Storks Tower Sauvignon Verdejo 2008** £5.99
Commercial but genuine modern brand has good grassy
Sauvignon character.

🍷9 **Finest Rueda 2008** £6.99
Excitingly flavoured melon-peach-gooseberry combo
with shining citrus finish.

SPARKLING WINES

FRANCE

🍷8 **Finest Vintage Champagne 2004** £19.95
For the extra money you get a rounder, creamier fizz than
the standard Tesco non-vintage. Gently appealing.

ITALY

🍷8 **La Gioiosa Prosecco Raboso Rosé
Spumante** £7.99
Lipstick-pink confection has lively mousse, sweet
strawberry fruit and lifting crispness. Naff but nice.

🍷9 **Finest Bisol Prosecco Valdobbiadene
Spumante** £8.99
Vigorously sparkly, and sweet in a convincingly Muscat-
grape sort of way, this has a nifty citrus counterpoint.
Best Prosecco of the year.

Waitrose

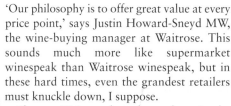

'Our philosophy is to offer great value at every price point,' says Justin Howard-Sneyd MW, the wine-buying manager at Waitrose. This sounds much more like supermarket winespeak than Waitrose winespeak, but in these hard times, even the grandest retailers must knuckle down, I suppose.

Phooey. Waitrose has always been in the first rank for wine among the supermarkets, and at prices that have never been other than fully competitive. In my two Top Tens of best buys under £4 for this special austerity edition, no fewer than six of the bargains are from Waitrose. No competitor comes close.

The range is enormous, and yes, it does include a lot of 'fine' wines – where else could you buy Vincent Girardin Meursault or Piancornello Brunello? But for sheer choice from one end of the scale to the other, there's nowhere like it. And there are so many quirky wines. At the huge 2009 tasting of 114 new wines and 134 new vintages, Justin Howard-Sneyd insisted I try an unheard-of rosé from the Peloponnese in Greece. 'Isn't it wonderful?' he enthused, as I squinted at the lurid colour and sniffed at the bubblegum nose. Yes, I liked it well enough, but what I really like is that a wine-buyer as talented and adventurous as this is at liberty to bring in such outlandish new lines – for a supermarket.

God bless Waitrose. And if you cannot find any of the 100 wines recommended here in your local branch, or wish to order in bulk, just look online at www.waitrose.com, where the entire list is featured and you can mix your own case for the minimum 12-bottle order. If the wines are on special offer, you get the same discount as you would in store.

RED WINES

Waitrose

ARGENTINA

8 **Familia Zuccardi FuZion**
Shiraz/Malbec 2008   **£4.49**
Sneaky caramel whiff and soft, plush fruit finished with a
tannin grip in this easy glugger.

8 **Otra Vida Merlot 2008**   **£5.99**
Plump, agreeably sweet sipping wine with a clean edge.

AUSTRALIA

8 **Plantagenet Samson's Range**
Shiraz/Cabernet 2007   **£7.99**
Fruitcake whiff from this generous (14.5% alcohol)
blend evokes Christmas; comforting and satisfying to
drink with meat or fowl.

8 **Katnook Founder's Block**
Cabernet Sauvignon 2006   **£8.99**
Dark and minty modestly weighted blackcurranty
Coonawarra in plush maturity.

9 **The Hedonist Shiraz 2006**   **£9.99**
I liked the pig on the label, and the creamy-spicy impact
and continuity of the piquant, juicy blackberry fruit.
Lovely McLaren Vale wine with 14% alcohol.

9 **Wirra Wirra Church Block 2007**   **£9.99**
Lush concentrated McLaren Vale Cabernet-Shiraz-
Merlot is dark but creamy and ideally weighted, wearing
its 14.5% alcohol lightly.

8 **Shelmerdine Pinot Noir 2008**   **£12.99**
Elegant, even delicate, light-bodied but crunchily bright
and firmly knit summer-pudding Pinot from the Yarra
Valley. Worth it.

RED WINES

CHILE

🍷8 **Virtue Merlot/Cabernet Sauvignon 2008**   £3.99
UK bottled in lightweight glass to save the planet, this gutsy blend has a fresh, almost green nose, spiced fruit and keen edge. Likeable.

🍷8 **Cousiño Macul Antiguas Reservas
Cabernet Sauvignon 2006**   £8.99
Elegant pure Cabernet from Chile's most aristocratic winery has claret-like cedar-tobacco nose but lush Chilean ripeness and 14% alcohol.

FRANCE

🍷9 **Cuvée Chasseur 2008**   £3.69
Big purple Hérault vin de pays has confected smell but bright, brambly healthy fruit finishing very correctly brisk. Convincing and very cheap.

🍷8 **Classic Côtes du Rhône 2008**   £3.99
Presumptuous name, and at the price you expect faults, but there are none: vivid, authentic, spicy red-fruit Grenache of good character.

🍷8 **Good Ordinary Claret 2007**   £3.99
A nice drop from the Entre Deux Mers wine lake, this is generous in Merlot fruit and good value.

🍷8 **Réserve de la Perrière 2008**   £3.99
Bright gripping spicy Corbières with black fruit and keen edge to drink with cassoulet.

🍷9 **Fitou Réserve de Courtal 2007**   £4.99
Unusually rounded pure-fruit plummy (Victoria, with skin on) food red with 14% alcohol. Long and spicy.

RED WINES

8 Waitrose Claret Reserve 2007 £5.29
Vigorously concentrated Merlot-led blend with evident oak and black-fruit sweetness.

8 La Baume Merlot 2008 £5.99
Big brand vin de pays d'Oc has Chilean-style elegance but is robust with blackberry fruitiness and 14.5% alcohol. Insinuating.

8 Saint Roche Vin de Pays du Gard 2008 £6.49
Big briary flavours and 14% alcohol with cinnamon note in a seven-grape blend with pleasantly abrading texture. Grilled meats will go well.

9 Saumur Les Nivières 2007 £6.49
Perennial favourite from the Loire is light, leafy and lively, fresh and cleansing and yet very firmly fruity and juicy; stands out a mile.

**8 Gérard Bertrand Grand Terroir
Tautavel 2006** £7.99
Sweetly ripe Roussillon from rugby legend Bertrand is plump, spicy and 14% alcohol, with a firm grip at the finish.

**9 Cellier des Dauphins Côtes du Rhône
Villages Vinsobres 2007** £8.99
Top wine under a ubiquitous brand is lusciously dense and squishy (and 14% alcohol) with spice in the background and sweet ripeness to the fore.

FRANCE

RED WINES

8 **Blason de Bourgogne Hautes**
Côtes de Nuits 2007 £9.99
Earthy-brown, spirity-nosed burgundy has silky-textured
classic Pinot summer-fruit. One of several Blason brand
wines that have really impressed this year.

8 **Bouchard Père et Fils Fleurie 2008** £9.99
Instantly appealing senior Beaujolais has juicy vigour and
substantial fruit with a white-pepper flourish. Classic but
pricy.

8 **Madiran Château d'Aydie 2006** £11.99
Fans of Madiran (the world's healthiest wine) will relish
this truffle-scented inky monster for its black heart and
cushy weight.

8 **Waitrose Châteauneuf du Pape**
Le Chemin des Mulets 2006 £19.99
Under the elusive Waitrose in Partnership label (with top
grower Perrin), a rarely good and approachable
Châteauneuf with ripe complexity and 14.5% alcohol.

8 **Château Larrivet Haut-Brion 2004** £23.50
Lovely mature-tasting claret from a grand Graves estate
has rich coffee notes, minty silkiness, good bones. Yes,
worth it – but cheaper (£19.99) at Majestic.

8 **Trinacria Rosso 2008** £3.99
'Sicilian sunshine' avers the back-label note, and I agree:
a brightly fruity bargain with Mediterranean herbal
notes.

FRANCE

ITALY

RED WINES

9 **Mezzomondo Negroamaro 2007** £4.99
From Salento in Puglia, a darkly ripe, briary-spicy food red (meaty pasta) with a luscious trace of liquorice.

7 **Bardolino Recchia 2008** £5.99
Cherry colour, smell and flavour with almondy finish, a decent example of a once-fashionable Veronese wine to drink cool.

9 **Sella & Mosca Capocaccia 2004** £6.99
From a leading Sardinian producer, a mature, browning Cannonau/Cabernet blend with Barolo-like spirty/rose-bloom scent and sweet-but-grippy flavour. The island in a glass!

8 **Conti Zecca Donna Marzia Primitivo 2006** £7.49
Wordy label boasts of a '*gusto morbido ed armonico*' which translates to me as an epic roasty but vivid, spicy Puglian comfort red with 14.5% alcohol and a nice coffee note.

9 **Chianti Poggiotando Cerro del Masso 2007** £7.99
Noticeably rich and velvety texture to this dense but proper cherry/raspberry Chianti. Unusually fair price.

8 **Cantina di Negrar Amarone della Valpolicella Classico 2006** £16.99
Nicely toasted (but not burnt) example of this built-up, bitter-sweet after-dinner (with cheese) oddity at 15% alcohol.

9 **Piancornello Brunello di Montalcino 2003** £25.00
Of merely academic interest I suppose, but a fabulous example of this grandest of Tuscan reds with sublime richness and purity of plump, minty fruit (and 14% alcohol).

ITALY

RED WINES

KOSOVO

6 **Stonecastle Premium Vranac 2007** £7.99
Middleweight Balkan red claims 'black forest fruit flavours' and is pleasantly finished by a twangy acidity, but too expensive.

LEBANON

8 **Château Ka Source de Rouge 2005** £10.99
So like its famed Bekaa Valley neighbour Chateau Musar, it's spooky. Quirky Cabernet-Merlot blend with spirity blackberry, spicy, coffee/cinnamon notes and 14% alcohol.

MONTENEGRO

7 **Plantaze Merlot 2006** £7.49
Dense maroon colour to this mature, nicely weighted Balkan black-cherry, Italian-style red with a spring in its step.

NEW ZEALAND

8 **Oyster Bay Pinot Noir 2007** £9.99
Classic slinky-eucalypt Marlborough with lush raspberry-and-cream flavours.

8 **Vidal Syrah 2007** £9.99
Dense maroon Hawkes Bay silky number has a highland-heather perfume, long, rich plummy flavours and 14% alcohol.

8 **Wild Rock Gravel Pit Red 2007** £9.99
Mostly Merlot, a deeply Kiwi spin on the grape's black-cherry character with minty-grippy finish. Perfect for roast beef.

RED WINES

N ZEALAND

9 **Wither Hills Pinot Noir 2007** £15.99
Absolutely bouncing Pinot fruit (14% alcohol) from revered Wairau estate is my favourite, except for the price. Mind you, preferred it to the Cloudy Bay at £5 more.

PORTUGAL

8 **Vida Nova Syrah-Aragonez 2007** £6.99
Cliff Richard's Algarve vineyard is on song with this plummy, even pruny, long-flavoured oaked red with a nice nutty edge; 14% alcohol.

8 **Cortes de Cima Syrah 2004** £9.99
Sweet-centred, near-raisiny Alentejo with silkiness and spice, and 14% alcohol.

7 **Quinta do Vallado Touriga Nacional 2006** £17.99
Lovely creamy yet peppery monster silky Douro red at 14% alcohol. Price seems steep though.

SOUTH AFRICA

9 **The Whale Caller Shiraz/ Cabernet Sauvignon 2008** £3.89
Eager, healthy blend with a nice tarry element is very cheap. Good with chili dishes.

8 **Zalze Shiraz/Mourvèdre/Viognier 2007** £5.99
Structured and very ripe (14.5% alcohol), with a hint of oloroso, a big friendly Stellenbosch blend to drink with venison or rare beef.

8 **Waitrose Foundation Shiraz 2008** £7.99
Part of the profit goes to the winery's local community; it's money well spent for a deeply dark wine with burnt-orange and toffee aroma and spiced blackberry fruit; 14% alcohol.

RED WINES

S AFRICA

8 **Southern Right Pinotage 2007** £11.99
Pinotage fans can invest with confidence in this classic sweet plummy keeping wine from Walker Bay, where Southern Right whales are to be seen.

SPAIN

8 **Don Simon Tempranillo** £3.49
Deep purple colour, porty smell and vivid brambly fruit, a shade stalky, to this Castillian cheapie. Likeable.

8 **Salduba Garnacha 2007** £4.99
Gripping blackcurrant Cariñena red to match starchy rice dishes such as paella.

8 **Mas Collet Celler de Capçanes 2005** £5.99
Followers of this perennial bargain might fail to recognise the radical new label; still the same dense, meaty, briary monster (14% alcohol) of memory, though. Good with duck.

9 **Jumilla Crianza Castillo San Simon 2006** £6.99
Fab mock-Rioja from Valencian hinterland has plush strawberries-and-cream freshness/richness. Really convincing.

10 **Barón de Ley Club Privado Reserva Rioja 2005** £7.99
The real thing: a rounded, perfectly ripe summer-fruit-plump Rioja with subtle vanilla, gentle tannic grip, lively acidity. Brilliant value.

8 **Torres Ibéricos Rioja Crianza 2006** £8.99
Penedes producer Torres's first venture into Rioja is earthy, almost austere, but authentic (and 14% alcohol).

PINK WINES

AUSTRALIA

🍷7 **St Hallett Rosé 2008** £6.99
Near-red, leafy-scented, fresh but plumply soft-fruited Grenache-Shiraz-Gewürztraminer Barossa blend. Oddly likeable.

🍷8 **Cuvée Fleur Rosé 2008** £3.79
Pale salmon colour, soft but clean-edged refresher with residual sweetness from Béziers, and impressively cheap.

🍷7 **Champteloup Selection Rosé d'Anjou 2008** £5.99
Shameless commercial Loire pink is sweet without being confected, finishing brisk.

🍷8 **Foncaussade Les Parcelles Rosé 2008** £6.49
From that well of mediocrity, Bergerac, a nonetheless delightful salmon-pink Merlot-Cabernet blend with brisk, fleshy fruit that really tastes pink.

FRANCE

🍷8 **Domaine de Buganay Rosé 2008** £7.99
Provence pink with orange hue, flinty aroma and matching restrained fruit; delicate and very refreshing.

🍷8 **Château d'Aqueria Rosé 2008** £9.79
Man's rosé (can I say that?) from Tavel in the Rhône is luminous magenta, exuberantly aromatic and full of juicy but crisp fruit.

🍷7 **Sancerre Joseph Mellot
La Demoiselle Rosé 2008** £11.99
Very nice but very expensive Loire classic is pure Pinot Noir but smells of Sauvignon Blanc; onion-skin colour, wildly fresh and mineral with strawberry airs and an amazing 14.5% alcohol.

PINK WINES

GREECE

7 **Skouras Rosé 2008** **£9.99**
Waitrose wine boss Justin Howard-Sneyd's pride and joy, this Peloponnesian pink has bubblegum charm. A Mama Mia wine.

MOLDOVA

8 **Firebird Legend Merlot Rosé 2008** **£4.99**
Coral colour, rose-bloom nose, generous sweet summer fruit, and good price.

PORTUGAL

8 **Vida Nova Rosé 2008** **£6.99**
Orange tinge, big floral nose and long, ripe flavours in this artful Algarve refresher from Cliff Richard's vineyards.

USA

7 **Fetzer Valley Oaks**
White Zinfandel Rosé 2007 **£6.99**
Big, juicy and exotic pink has a well-contrived sweetness that fills a place in the market; just 11% alcohol.

WHITE WINES

AUSTRALIA

10 **De Bortoli Verdelho 2008** **£5.99**
Lovely fruit-salad dry Riverina white stands out a mile for its balance between exciting flavours and power to refresh. The price refreshes too. Why can't more Aussie wines be like this?

8 **Henschke Louis Semillon 2007** **£12.99**
Lavish tropical-fruit food wine (asparagus, salmon) has sumptuous weight but finishes perfectly dry.

CHILE

10 **Virtue Sauvignon Blanc/Chardonnay 2008** **£3.99**
Environmentally friendly, UK-bottled (in light glass) blend, amazingly, tastes clearly of its distinct constituent grape varieties and is thrillingly fruity and fresh. Terrific bargain.

8 **Errazuriz Max Reserva Chardonnay 2007** **£8.99**
Ripe yellow de luxe peachy Chardonnay enriched with toasty oak is unsubtle but deeply reassuring, and 14% alcohol.

8 **Waitrose Chilean Sauvignon Blanc 2008** **£8.99**
Luxury Sauvignon is plush but tangy, an unusual style that merits trying.

ENGLAND

6 **Chapel Down Flint Dry 2008** **£7.49**
Waitrose valiantly supports English wine; this Kentish one is not flint dry, but is pleasantly refreshing. Price not warranted, though.

WHITE WINES

7 Cuvée Pêcheur 2008   **£3.99**
Eager-to-please, crisp, dry Gascon white is just short of green; 11.5% alcohol.

**8 La Chasse du Pape Chardonnay/
Viognier 2008**   **£5.99**
Ubiquitous brand, but none the worse for that, this vin de pays d'Oc is attractively busy with peach-pineapple fruit and bright with limey freshness.

8 La Vieille Ferme 2008   **£5.99**
Established Luberon (Provence) brand is sunny-ripe with a nice cabbagey crispness atop the mellow peachy fruit.

**9 Le Fief Guérin Muscadet
Côtes de Grandlieu Sur Lie 2008**   **£5.99**
Muscadet of grand provenance crams in lots of racy briny fruit and crisp zest; as good as this Loire favourite gets.

**7 Champteloup Selection
Sauvignon Blanc 2008**   **£6.49**
Grassy but craftily sweet Loire crowd-pleaser.

8 Saumur Les Andides 2008   **£6.49**
Attractive spearmint note in this tangy Loire aperitif dry white.

8 Domaine Félines Picpoul de Pinet 2008   **£6.99**
Well-coloured, snappy-fresh Mediterranean seafood matcher with more body than usual.

FRANCE

WHITE WINES

8   Louis Jadot Mâcon-Azé 2007   **£8.99**
Dramatic gold colour, rich ripe Chardonnay fruit (but unoaked) lingers long; good old-fashioned burgundy.

9   Château Jolys Cuvée St Jean 2006   **£10.99**
From Pyrenees AC of Jurançon, a lavish, gold-bullion-coloured 'dessert' wine with nectar nose, honeyed fruit and fine balance of citrus acidity; a match, too, for foie gras or strong blue cheeses.

7   Masson-Blondelet Pouilly-Fumé 2007   **£12.49**
Yellow colour, lush Sauvignon fruit and pebbly freshness. So good, but so pricy.

**9   Pernand-Vergelesses Jean-Jacques
      Girard les Belles-Filles 2007**   **£14.99**
From the forest of burgundies this jumped out: rich, toasty-oaked but brightly mineral peachy-creamy Chardonnay coalesces into pefect fruit-freshness balance. Lush and worth the price.

9   Château Doisy Daëne 2005 37.5cl   **£16.49**
A sublime Sauternes already drinking beautifully: ambrosial. An experience, at a price.

**8   Vincent Girardin Meursault
      Le Limozin 2006**   **£29.00**
Just for the sake of the record, if it must be Meursault, go for this one. Ravishingly lush, nutty and balanced. The price must simply be borne.

FRANCE

WHITE WINES

GREECE

8 **Anthemis Muscat of Samos 2002 37.5cl** £9.99
Oloroso colour, honey aroma, grapy sweetness with fruitcake complexity; great aperitif with a light touch, despite 15% alcohol.

ITALY

8 **Trinacria Bianco 2008** £3.99
Light and fresh Sicilian with a touch of brimstone.

8 **Italia Grillo 2008** £5.99
Plainly packaged but deliciously nutty and refreshing Sicilian grassy aperitif white.

8 **Monteforte Soave 2007** £6.99
Verona's classic white is a little infra dig these days, but this is a lovely generous example with almondy richness and sleek, racy fruit.

9 **Sant'Elisa Friulano 2008** £6.99
Hugely flavoursome off-dry wine from Tocai Friulano grape has tropical background to long, long tangy fruit. Great with fish, and Gorgonzola.

8 **Storie di Vite Pinot Grigio 2007** £6.99
From sub-Alpine Trentino, a hefty, smoky-spicy PG resembling the Alsace style. Way above average.

8 **Malvira Roero Arneis 2008** £9.99
Lemon-gold Piedmont food wine (pasta and pollo) is pure, sleek, almondy and very Italian.

WHITE WINES

NEW ZEALAND

7 **Waitrose Sauvignon Blanc 2008** £8.49
Made by Villa Maria, it's crisp, grassy, briny and long-flavoured but no cheaper than the branded wine.

8 **Cloudy Bay Chardonnay 2007** £19.99
Cult brand is lush, mineral and long (and 14% alcohol), so if you can bear to pay for the name, you won't be disappointed.

SOUTH AFRICA

8 **The Whale Caller Sauvignon Blanc/ Colombard 2008** £3.89
Daisy-fresh and tangy but well-built party wine.

7 **Zalze Chenin Blanc 2008** £5.99
Honeyed background to the flavour of this zesty 14% alcohol aperitif wine.

8 **Waitrose Foundation Chenin Blanc 2008** £7.99
Good-cause wine had me guessing at the mystery smell and flavour: fennel, celery or rhubarb maybe. Very nuanced and attractive slyly rich dry white.

8 **Deetlets Famille Semillon 2006** £18.99
Akin to the dry wine of a good Sauternes estate, this is yellow and extravagantly lush with pineapple, peach and sweet melon fruit and yet quite dry. Great treat.

SPAIN

8 **Gran Lopez Airen/Sauvignon Blanc 2008** £3.99
La Mancha party white with floral nose, soft but bright fruit and 11% alcohol.

FORTIFIED WINES

 **Quinta do Noval
10-Year-Old Tawny Port**   £15.99
Copper-coloured wood-aged port of silky texture and long, fruitcake flavours is my pick of the 10-year-old tawnies, in a field with very high standards. Try it cool.

 Gran Barquero Pedro Ximenez 50cl   £7.49
A fabulous Montilla with the sheen and colour of a newly popped conker, Christmas-cake aroma and richly sweet fruit evoking figs, raisins and roasted hazelnuts; drink with strong cheese – or chocoate. A revelation.

 **Waitrose Solera Jerezana Palo
Cortado Sherry**   £7.99
Sublime deep-amber, dry, nutty and limpid wine of great quality for true sherry aficionados is underpriced. All the others in this range, especially the amontillado and oloroso, score equally high.

SPARKLING WINES

Denbies Whitedowns Sparkling 2004   £15.99
Really likeable honey-toned, off-dry and fresh Surrey sparkler with a style of its own. Really clever stuff, and the price just about fits.

Bookers Sirius Sparkling Rosé   £17.95
Pale genteel pink fizz from Sussex has vigorous orchard-fruit flavours and good acidity, but it's expensive for what it is.

SPARKLING WINES

FRANCE

8 **Crémant de Limoux Cuvée Royale Brut** £8.99
Expressive Chardonnay-led blend from underrated Pyrenees AC is ripe, not sweet, with good mousse.

10 **Crémant de Bourgogne Cave de Lugny Blanc de Blancs** £9.99
Sparkling burgundy can come close to champagne in style and this pure Chardonnay does it convincingly. Super value.

8 **Alexandre Bonnet Champagne Brut Rosé** £24.99
Coral colour, sweet-smelling, strawberry-ripe plump fruit; rather sexy.

USA

7 **Roederer Estate Quartet Brut** £19.99
It looks, smells and tastes like champagne, but it's from a vineyard owned by top Reims house Louis Roederer. What are they doing?

What wine words
—mean—

Wine labels are getting crowded. It's mostly thanks to the unending torrent of new regulation. In the last couple of years, for example, the European Union has decided that all wines sold within its borders must display a health warning: 'Contains Sulphites'. All wines are made with the aid of preparations containing sulphur to combat diseases in the vineyards and bacterial infections in the winery. You can't make wine without sulphur. Even 'organic' wines are made with it. But some people are sensitive to the traces of sulphur in some wines, so we must all be informed of the presence of this hazardous material.

That's the way it is. And it might not be long before some even sterner warnings will be added about another ingredient in wine. Alcohol is the new tobacco, as the regulators see it, and in the near future we can look forward to some stiff admonishments about the effects of alcohol. In the meantime, the mandatory information on every label includes the quantity, alcoholic strength and country of origin, along with the name of the producer. The region will be specified, vaguely on wines from loosely regulated countries such as Australia, and precisely on wines from over-regulated countries such as France. Wines from 'classic' regions of Europe – Bordeaux, Chianti, Rioja and so on – are mostly labelled according to their location rather than their constituent grape varieties. If it says Sancerre, it's taken as read that you either know it's made with Sauvignon Blanc grapes, or don't care.

Wines from just about everywhere else make no such assumptions. If a New Zealand wine is made from Sauvignon Blanc grapes, you can be sure the label will say so. This does quite neatly represent the gulf between the two worlds of winemaking. In traditional European regions, it's the place, the vineyard, that mostly determines the character of the wines. The French call it terroir, to encapsulate not just the lie of the land and the soil conditions but the wild variations in the weather from year to year as well. The grapes are merely the medium through which the timeless mysteries of the deep earth are translated into the ineffable glories of the wine, adjusted annually according to the vagaries of climate, variable moods of the winemaker, and who knows what else.

In the less arcane vineyards of the New World, the grape is definitely king. In hot valleys such as the Barossa (South Australia) or the Maipo (Chile) valleys, climate is relatively predictable and the soil conditions are managed by irrigation. It's the fruit that counts, and the style of the wine is determined by the variety – soft, spicy Shiraz; peachy, yellow Chardonnay and so on.

The main purpose of this glossary is, consequently, to give short descriptions of the 'classic' wines, including the names of the grapes they are made from, and of the 70-odd distinct grape varieties that make most of the world's wines. As well as these very brief descriptions, I have included equally shortened summaries of the regions and appellations of the better-known wines, along with some of the local terms used to indicate style and alleged qualities.

Finally, I have tried to explain in simple and rational terms the peculiar words I use in trying to convey the characteristics of wines described. 'Delicious' might need no further qualification, but the likes of 'bouncy', 'green' and 'liquorous' probably do.

A

abboccato – Medium-dry white wine style. Italy, especially Orvieto.

AC – *See* Appellation d'Origine Contrôlée.

acidity – To be any good, every wine must have the right level of acidity. It gives wine the element of dryness or sharpness it needs to prevent cloying sweetness or dull wateriness. If there is too much acidity, wine tastes raw or acetic (vinegary). Winemakers strive to create balanced acidity – either by cleverly controlling the natural processes, or by adding sugar and acid to correct imbalances.

aftertaste – The flavour that lingers in the mouth after swallowing the wine.

Aglianico – Black grape variety of southern Italy. It has romantic associations. When the ancient Greeks first colonised Italy in the seventh century BC, it was with the prime purpose of planting it as a vineyard (the Greek name for Italy was *Oenotria* – land of cultivated vines). The name for the vines the Greeks brought with them was Ellenico (as in Hellas, Greece), from which Aglianico is the modern rendering. To return to the point, these ancient vines, especially in the arid volcanic landscapes of Basilicata and Cilento, produce excellent dark, earthy and highly distinctive wines. A name to look out for.

Agriculture biologique – On French wine labels, an indication that the wine has been made by organic methods.

Albariño – White grape variety of Spain that makes intriguingly perfumed fresh and spicy dry wines, especially in esteemed Rias Baixas region.

alcohol – The alcohol levels in wines are expressed in terms of alcohol by volume ('abv'), that is, the percentage of the volume of the wine that is common, or ethyl, alcohol. A typical wine at 12 per cent abv is thus 12 parts alcohol and, in effect, 88 parts fruit juice.

The question of how much alcohol we can drink without harming ourselves in the short or long term is an impossible one to answer, but there is more or less general agreement among scientists that small amounts of alcohol are good for us, even if the only evidence of this is actuarial – the fact that mortality statistics show teetotallers live significantly shorter lives than moderate drinkers. According to the Department of Health, there are 'safe limits' to the amount of alcohol we should drink weekly. These limits are measured in units of alcohol, with a small glass of wine taken to be one unit. Men are advised that 28 units a week is the most they can drink without risk to health, and for women (whose liver function differs from that of men because of metabolic differences) the figure is 21 units.

If you wish to measure your consumption closely, note that a standard 75 cl bottle of wine at 12 per cent alcohol contains 9 units. A bottle of German Moselle at 8 per cent alcohol has only 6 units, but a bottle of Australian Chardonnay at 14 per cent has 10.5.

Alentejo – Wine region of southern Portugal (immediately north of the Algarve), with a fast-improving reputation, especially for sappy, keen reds from local grape varieties including Aragones, Castelão and Trincadeira grapes.

Almansa – DO winemaking region of Spain inland from Alicante, making great-value red wines.

Alsace – France's easternmost wine-producing region lies between the Vosges Mountains and the River Rhine, with Germany beyond. These conditions make for the production of some of the world's most delicious and fascinating white wines, always sold under the name of their constituent grapes. Pinot Blanc is the most affordable – and is well worth looking out for. The 'noble' grape varieties of the region are Gewürztraminer, Muscat, Riesling and Tokay Pinot Gris and they are always made on a single-variety basis. The richest, most exotic wines are those from individual *grand cru* vineyards, which are named on the label. Some *vendange tardive* (late harvest) wines are made, but tend to be expensive. All the wines are sold in tall, slim green bottles known as flûtes that closely resemble those of the Mosel, and the names of producers and grape varieties are often German too, so it is widely assumed that Alsace wines are German in style, if not in nationality. But this is not the case in either particular. Alsace wines are dry and quite unique in character – and definitely French.

Amarone – Style of red wine made in Valpolicella, Italy. Specially selected grapes are held back from the harvest and stored for several months to dry them out. They are then pressed and fermented into a highly concentrated speciality dry wine. Amarone means 'bitter', describing the dry style of the flavour.

amontillado – *See* Sherry.

aperitif – If a wine is thus described, I believe it will give more pleasure before a meal than with one. Crisp, low-alcohol German wines and other delicately flavoured whites (including many dry Italians) are examples.

Appellation d'Origine Contrôlée – Commonly abbreviated to AC or AOC, this is the system under which quality wines are defined in France. About a third of the country's vast annual output qualifies, and there are more than 400 distinct AC zones. The declaration of an AC on the label signifies that the wine meets standards concerning location of vineyards and wineries, grape varieties and limits on harvest per hectare, methods of cultivation and vinification, and alcohol content. Wines are inspected and tasted by state-appointed committees. The one major aspect of any given wine that an AC cannot guarantee is that you will like it – but it certainly improves the chances.

Apulia – Anglicised name for Puglia.

Ardèche – Region of southern France to the west of the Rhône valley, home to a good vin de pays zone known as the Coteaux de L'Ardèche. Lots of decent-value reds from Syrah grapes, and some, less interesting, dry whites.

Assyrtiko – White grape variety of Greece now commonly named on dry white wines, sometimes of great quality, from the mainland and islands.

Asti – Town and major winemaking centre in Piedmont, Italy. The sparkling (spumante) sweet wines made from Moscato grapes are inexpensive and often delicious. Typical alcohol level is a modest 5 to 7 per cent.

attack – In wine tasting, the first impression made by the wine in the mouth.

Auslese – German wine-quality designation. *See* QmP.

B

Baga – Black grape variety indigenous to Portugal. Makes famously concentrated, juicy reds that get their deep colour from the grape's particularly thick skins. Look out for this name, now quite frequently quoted as the varietal on Portuguese wine labels. Often very good value for money.

balance – A big word in the vocabulary of wine tasting. Respectable wine must get two key things right: lots of fruitiness from the sweet grape juice, and plenty of acidity so the sweetness is 'balanced' with the crispness familiar in good dry whites and the dryness that marks out good reds. Some wines are noticeably 'well balanced' in that they have memorable fruitiness and the clean, satisfying 'finish' (last flavour in the mouth) that ideal acidity imparts.

Barbera – Black grape variety originally of Piedmont in Italy. Most commonly seen as Barbera d'Asti, the vigorously fruity red wine made around Asti – which is better known for sweet sparkling Asti Spumante. Barbera grapes are now being grown in South America, often producing a sleeker, smoother style than at home in Italy.

Bardolino – Once fashionable, light red wine DOC of Veneto, north-west Italy. Bardolino is made principally from Corvina Veronese grapes plus Rondinella, Molinara and Negrara. Best wines are supposed to be those labelled *classico*, and *superiore* is applied to those aged a year and having at least 11.5 per cent alcohol.

Barossa Valley – Famed vineyard region north of Adelaide, Australia, produces hearty reds principally from Shiraz, Cabernet Sauvignon and Grenache grapes, plus plenty of lush white wine from Chardonnay. Also known for limey, long-lived, mineral dry whites from Riesling grapes.

barrique – Barrel in French. *En barrique* on a wine label signifies the wine has been matured in oak.

Beaujolais – Unique red wines from the southern reaches of Burgundy, France, are made from Gamay grapes. Beaujolais nouveau, now deeply unfashionable, provides a friendly introduction to the bouncy, red-fruit style of the wine, but for the authentic experience, go for Beaujolais Villages, from the region's better, northern vineyards. There are ten AC zones within this northern sector making wines under their own names. Known as the crus, these are Brouilly, Chénas, Chiroubles, Côte de Brouilly, Fleurie, Juliénas, Morgon, Moulin à Vent, Regnié and St Amour and produce most of the best wines of the region. Prices are higher than those for Beaujolais Villages, but by no means always justifiably so.

Beaumes de Venise – Village near Châteauneuf du Pape in France's Rhône valley, famous for sweet and alcoholic wine from Muscat grapes. Delicious, grapey wines. A small number of growers also make strong (sometimes rather tough) red wines under the village name.

Beaune – One of the two winemaking centres (the other is Nuits St Georges) at the heart of Burgundy in France. Three of the region's humbler appellations take the name of the town: Côtes de Beaune, Côtes de Beaune Villages and Hautes Côtes de Beaune. Wines made under these ACs are often, but by no means always, good value for money.

berry fruit – Some red wines deliver a burst of flavour in the mouth that corresponds to biting into a newly picked berry – strawberry, blackberry, etc. So a wine described as having berry fruit (by this writer, anyway) has freshness, liveliness, immediate appeal.

bianco – White wine, Italy.

Bical – White grape variety principally of Dão region of northern Portugal. Not usually identified on labels, because most of it goes into inexpensive sparkling wines. Can make still wines of very refreshing crispness.

biodynamics – A cultivation method taking the organic approach several steps further. Biodynamic winemakers plant and tend their vineyards according to a date and time calendar 'in harmony' with the movements of the planets. Some of France's best-known wine estates subscribe, and many more are going that way. It might all sound bonkers, but it's salutary to learn that biodynamics is based on principles first described by a very eminent man, the Austrian educationist Rudolf Steiner. He's lately been in the news for having written, in 1919, that farmers crazy enough to feed animal products to cattle would drive the livestock 'mad'.

bite – In wine tasting, the impression on the palate of a wine with plenty of acidity and, often, tannin.

blanc – White wine, France.

blanc de blancs – White wine from white grapes, France. May seem to be stating the obvious, but some white wines (e.g. champagne) are made, partially or entirely, from black grapes.

blanc de noirs – White wine from black grapes, France. Usually sparkling (especially champagne) made from black Pinot Meunier and Pinot Noir grapes, with no Chardonnay or other white varieties.

blanco – White wine, Spain and Portugal.

Blauer Zweigelt – Black grape variety of Austria, making a large proportion of the country's red wines, some of excellent quality.

Bobal – Black grape variety mostly of south-eastern Spain. Thick skin is good for colour and juice contributes acidity to blends.

bodega – In Spain, a wine producer or wine shop.

Bonarda – Black grape variety of northern Italy. Now more widely planted in Argentina, where it makes rather elegant red wines, often representing great value.

botrytis – Full name, *botrytis cinerea*, is that of a beneficent fungus that can attack ripe grape bunches late in the season, shrivelling the berries to a gruesome-looking mess, which yields concentrated juice of prized sweetness. Cheerfully known as 'noble rot', this fungus is actively encouraged by winemakers in regions as diverse as Sauternes (in Bordeaux), Monbazillac (in Bergerac), the Rhine and Mosel valleys and South Australia to make ambrosial dessert wines.

bouncy – The feel in the mouth of a red wine with young, juicy fruitiness. Good Beaujolais is bouncy, as are many north-west-Italian wines from Barbera and Dolcetto grapes.

Bourgogne Grand Ordinaire – Appellation of France's Burgundy region for 'ordinary' red wines from either Gamay or Pinot Noir grapes, or both. Some good-value wines, especially from the Buxy co-operative in the southern Chalonnais area.

Bourgueil – Appellation of Loire Valley, France. Long-lived red wines from Cabernet Franc grapes.

briary – In wine-tasting, associated with the flavours of fruit from prickly bushes such as blackberries.

brûlé – Pleasant burnt-toffee taste or smell, as in crème brûlée.

brut – Driest style of sparkling wine. Originally French, for very dry champagnes specially developed for the British market, but now used for sparkling wines from all round the world.

Buzet – Little-seen AC of south-west France overshadowed by Bordeaux but producing some characterful ripe reds.

C

Cabardès – Recent AC (1998) for red and rosé wines from area north of Carcassonne, Aude, France. Principally Cabernet Sauvignon and Merlot grapes.

Cabernet Franc – Black grape variety originally of France. It makes the light-bodied and keenly-edged red wines of the Loire Valley – such as Chinon and Saumur. And it is much grown in Bordeaux, especially in the appellation of St Emilion. Also now planted in Argentina, Australia and North America. Wines, especially in the Loire, are characterised by a leafy, sappy style and bold fruitiness. Most are best enjoyed young.

Cabernet Sauvignon – Black (or, rather, blue) grape variety now grown in virtually every wine-producing nation. When perfectly ripened, the grapes are smaller than many other varieties and have particularly thick skins. This means that when pressed, Cabernet grapes have a high proportion of skin to juice – and that makes for wine with lots of colour and tannin. In Bordeaux, the grape's traditional home, the grandest Cabernet-based wines have always been known as *vins de garde* (wines to keep) because they take years, even decades, to evolve as the effect of all that skin extraction preserves the fruit all the way to magnificent maturity. But in today's impatient world, these grapes are exploited in modern winemaking techniques to produce the sublime flavours of mature Cabernet without having to hang around for lengthy periods awaiting maturation. While there's nothing like a fine, ten-year-old claret (and nothing quite as expensive), there are many excellent Cabernets from around the world that amply illustrate this grape's characteristics. Classic smells and flavours include blackcurrants, cedar wood, chocolate, tobacco – even violets.

Cahors – An AC of the Lot Valley in south-west France once famous for 'black wine'. This was a curious concoction of straightforward wine mixed with a soupy must, made by boiling up new-pressed juice to concentrate it (through evaporation) before fermentation. The myth is still perpetuated that Cahors wine continues to be made in this way, but production on this basis actually ceased 150 years ago. Cahors today is no stronger, or blacker, than the wines of neighbouring appellations.

Cairanne – Village of the appellation collectively known as the Côtes du Rhône Villages in southern France. Cairanne is one of several villages entitled to put their name on the labels of wines made within their AC boundary, and the appearance of this name is quite reliably an indicator of a very good wine indeed.

Calatayud – DO (quality wine zone) near Zaragoza in the Aragon region of northern Spain where they're making some astonishingly good wines at bargain prices, mainly reds from Garnacha and Tempranillo grapes. These are the varieties that go into the light and oaky wines of Rioja, but in Calatayud, the wines are dark, dense and decidedly different.

Cannonau – Black grape native to Sardinia by name, but in fact the same variety as the ubiquitous Grenache of France (and Garnacha of Spain).

cantina sociale – *See* Co-op.

Carignan – Black grape variety of Mediterranean France. It is rarely identified on labels, but is a major constituent of wines from the southern Rhône and Languedoc-Roussillon regions. Known as Carignano in Italy and Cariñena in Spain.

Cariñena – A region of north-east Spain, south of Navarra, known for substantial reds, as well as the Spanish name for the Carignan grape (*qv*).

Carmenère – Black grape variety once widely grown in Bordeaux but abandoned due to cultivation problems. Lately revived in South America where it is producing fine wines, sometimes with echoes of Bordeaux.

cassis – As a tasting note, signifies a wine that has a noticeable blackcurrant-concentrate flavour or smell. Much associated with the Cabernet Sauvignon grape.

Castelao – Portuguese black grape variety. Same as Periquita.

Catarratto – White grape variety of Sicily. In skilled hands it can make anything from keen, green-fruit dry whites to lush, oaked super-ripe styles. Also used for Marsala.

cat's pee – In tasting notes, a mildly jocular reference to a certain style of Sauvignon Blanc wine.

cava – The sparkling wine of Spain. Most originates in Catalonia, but the Denominación de Origen (DO) guarantee of authenticity is open to producers in many regions of the country. Much cava is very reasonably priced even though it is made by the same method as champagne – second fermentation in bottle, known in Spain as the *método clásico*.

CdR – Côtes du Rhône.

Cépage – Grape variety, French. 'Cépage Merlot' on a label simply means the wine is made largely or exclusively from Merlot grapes.

Chablis – Northernmost AC of France's Burgundy region. Its dry white wines from Chardonnay grapes are known for their fresh and steely style, but the best wines also age very gracefully into complex classics.

Chambourcin – Sounds like a cream cheese but it's a relatively modern (1963) French hybrid black grape that makes some good non-appellation lightweight-but-concentrated reds in the Loire Valley and now some heftier versions in Australia.

Chardonnay – The world's most popular grape variety. Said to originate from the village of Chardonnay in the Mâconnais region of southern Burgundy, the vine is now planted in every wine-producing nation. Wines are commonly characterised by generous colour and sweet-apple smell, but styles range from lean and sharp to opulently rich. Australia started the craze for oaked Chardonnay, the gold-coloured, super-ripe, buttery 'upfront' wines that are a caricature of lavish and outrageously expensive burgundies such as Meursault and Puligny-Montrachet. Rich to the point of egginess, these Aussie pretenders are now giving way to a sleeker, more minerally style with much less oak presence – if any at all. California and Chile, New Zealand and South Africa are competing hard to imitate the Burgundian style, and Australia's success in doing so.

Châteauneuf du Pape – Famed appellation centred on a picturesque village of the southern Rhône valley in France where in the 1320s French Pope Clement V had a splendid new château built for himself as a country retreat amidst his vineyards. The red wines of the AC, which can be made from 13 different grape varieties but principally Grenache, Syrah and Mourvèdre, are regarded as the best of the southern Rhône and have become rather expensive – but they can be sensationally good. Expensive white wines are also made.

Chenin blanc – White grape variety of the Loire Valley, France. Now also grown farther afield, especially in South Africa. Makes dry, soft white wines and also rich, sweet styles. Sadly, many low-cost Chenin wines are bland and uninteresting.

cherry – In wine tasting, either a pale red colour or, more commonly, a smell or flavour akin to the sun-warmed, bursting sweet ripeness of cherries. Many Italian wines, from lightweights such as Bardolino and Valpolicella to serious Chianti, have this character. 'Black cherry' as a description is often used of Merlot wines – meaning they are sweet but have a firmness associated with the thicker skins of black cherries.

Cinsault – Black grape variety of southern France, where it is invariably blended with others in wines of all qualities ranging from vin de pays to the pricy reds of Châteauneuf du Pape. Also much planted in South Africa. The effect in wine is to add keen aromas (sometimes compared with turpentine!) and softness to the blend. The name is often spelt Cinsaut.

Clape, La – A small cru (defined quality-vineyard area) within the Coteaux du Languedoc where the growers make some seriously delicious red wines, mainly from Carignan, Grenache and Syrah grapes. A name worth looking out for on labels from the region.

claret – The red wine of Bordeaux, France. It comes from Latin *clarus*, meaning 'clear', recalling a time when the red wines of the region were much lighter in colour than they are now.

clarete – On Spanish labels indicates a pale-coloured red wine. Tinto signifies a deeper hue.

classed growth – English translation of French *cru classé* describes a group of 60 individual wine estates in the Médoc district of Bordeaux, which in 1855 were granted this new status on the basis that their wines were the most expensive at that time. The classification was a promotional wheeze to attract attention to the Bordeaux stand at that year's Great Exhibition in Paris. Amazingly, all of the 60 wines concerned are still in production and most still occupy more or less their original places in the pecking order price-wise. The league was divided up into five divisions from Premier Grand Cru Classé (just four wines originally, with one promoted in 1971 – the only change ever made to the classification) to Cinquième Grand Cru Classé. Other regions of Bordeaux, notably Graves and St Emilion, have since imitated Médoc and introduced their own rankings of *cru classé* estates.

classic – An overused term in every respect – wine descriptions being no exception. In this book, the word is used to describe a very good wine of its type. So, a 'classic' Cabernet Sauvignon is one that is recognisably and admirably characteristic of that grape.

Classico – Under Italy's wine laws, this word appended to the name of a DOC zone has an important significance. The classico wines of the region can only be made from vineyards lying in the best-rated areas, and wines thus labelled (e.g. Chianti Classico, Soave Classico, Valpolicella Classico) can be reliably counted on to be a cut above the rest.

Colombard – White grape variety of southern France. Once employed almost entirely for making the wine that is distilled for armagnac and cognac brandies, but lately restored to varietal prominence in the Vin de Pays des Côtes de Gascogne where high-tech wineries turn it into a fresh and crisp, if unchallenging, dry wine at a budget price. But beware, cheap Colombard (especially from South Africa) can still be very dull.

Conca de Barbera – Winemaking region of Catalonia, Spain.

co-op – Very many of France's good-quality, inexpensive wines are made by co-operatives. These are wine-producing factories whose members, and joint-owners, are local *vignerons* (vine growers). Each year they sell their harvests to the co-op for turning into branded wines. In Italy, co-op wines can be identified by the words *Cantina Sociale* on the label and in Germany by the term *Winzergenossenschaft*.

Corbières – A name to look out for. It's an AC of France's Midi (deep south) and produces countless robust reds and a few interesting whites, often at bargain prices.

Cortese – White grape variety of Piedmont, Italy. At its best, makes amazingly delicious, keenly brisk and fascinating wines, including those of the Gavi DOCG. Worth seeking out.

Costières de Nîmes – Until 1989, this AC of southern France was known as the Costières de Gard. It forms a buffer between the southern Rhône and Languedoc-Roussillon regions, and makes wines from broadly the same range of grape varieties. It's a name to look out for, the best red wines being notable for their concentration of colour and fruit, with the earthy-spiciness of the better Rhône wines and a likeable liquorice note. A few good white wines, too, and even a decent rosé or two.

Côte – In French, it simply means a side, or slope, of a hill. The implication in wine terms is that the grapes come from a vineyard ideally situated for maximum sunlight, good drainage and the unique soil conditions prevailing on the hill in question. It's fair enough to claim that vines grown on slopes might get more sunlight than those grown on the flat, but there is no guarantee whatsoever that any wine labelled 'Côtes du' this or that is made from grapes grown on a hillside anyway. Côtes du Rhône wines are a case in point. Many 'Côtes' wines come from entirely level vineyards and it is worth remembering that many of the vineyards of Bordeaux, producing most of the world's priciest wines, are little short of prairie-flat. The quality factor is determined much more significantly by the weather and the talents of the winemaker.

Côtes de Blaye – Appellation Contrôlée zone of Bordeaux on the right bank of the River Gironde, opposite the more prestigious Médoc zone of the left bank. A couple of centuries ago, Blaye (pronounced 'bligh') was the grander of the two, and even today makes some wines that compete well for quality, and at a fraction of the price of wines from its more fashionable rival across the water.

Côtes du Luberon – Appellation Contrôlée zone of Provence in southeast France. Wines, mostly red, are similar in style to Côtes du Rhône.

Côtes du Rhône – One of the biggest and best-known appellations of south-east France, covering an area roughly defined by the southern reaches of the valley of the River Rhône. Long notorious for cheap and execrable reds, the Côtes du Rhône AC has lately achieved remarkable improvements in quality at all points along the price scale. Lots of brilliant-value warm and spicy reds, principally from Grenache and Syrah grapes. There are also some white and rosé wines. Note that this region has had a brilliant run of vintages from 2004, with 2005 and 2006 particularly good and 2007 better than other regions in a difficult year for France as a whole.

Côtes du Rhône Villages – Appellation within the larger Côtes du Rhône AC for wine of supposed superiority made in a number of zones associated with a long list of nominated individual villages. Villages wines may be more interesting than their humbler counterparts, but this cannot be counted on. Go for the 2005 vintage if you can find any.

Côtes du Roussillon – Huge appellation of south-west France known for strong, dark, peppery reds often offering very decent value.

Côtes du Roussillon Villages – Appellation for superior wines from a number of nominated locations within the larger Roussillon AC. Some of these village wines can be of exceptional quality and value.

crianza – Means 'nursery' in Spanish. On Rioja and Navarra wines, the designation signifies a wine that has been nursed through a maturing period of at least a year in oak casks and a further six months in bottle before being released for sale.

cru – A word that crops up with confusing regularity on French wine labels. It means 'the growing' or 'the making' of a wine and asserts that the wine concerned is from a specific vineyard. Under the Appellation Contrôlée rules, countless crus are classified in various hierarchical ranks. Hundreds of individual vineyards are described as premier cru or grand cru in the classic wine regions of Alsace, Bordeaux, Burgundy and Champagne. The common denominator is that the wine can be counted on to be enormously expensive. On humbler wines, the use of the word cru tends to be mere decoration.

cru classé – *See* classed growth.

cuve – A vat for wine. French.

cuvée – French for the wine in a cuve, or vat. The word is much used on labels to imply that the wine is from just one vat, and thus of unique, unblended character. Première cuvée is supposedly the best wine from a given pressing because the grapes have had only the initial, gentle squashing to extract the free-run juice. Subsequent cuvées will have been from harsher pressings, grinding the grape pulp to extract the last drop of juice.

D

Dão – Major wine-producing region of northern Portugal now turning out much more interesting reds than it used to – worth looking out for anything made by mega-producer Sogrape.

demi sec – 'Half-dry' style of French (and some other) wines. Beware. It can mean anything from off-dry to cloyingly sweet.

DO – Denominación de Origen, Spain's wine-regulating scheme, similar to France's AC, but older – the first DO region was Rioja, from 1926. DO wines are Spain's best, accounting for a third of the nation's annual production.

DOC – Stands for Denominazione di Origine Controllata, Italy's equivalent of France's AC. The wines are made according to the stipulations of each of its 280 denominated zones of origin, 20 of which enjoy the superior classification of DOCG (DOC with *e Garantita* – guaranteed – appended).

Durif – Rare black grape variety mostly of California, where it is also known as Petite Sirah, but with some plantings in Australia.

E

earthy – A tricky word in the wine vocabulary. In this book, its use is meant to be complimentary. It indicates that the wine somehow suggests the soil the grapes were grown in, even (perhaps a shade too poetically) the landscape in which the vineyards lie. The amazing-value red wines of the torrid, volcanic southernmost regions of Italy are often described as earthy. This is an association with the pleasantly 'scorched' back-flavour in wines made from the ultra-ripe harvests of this near-sub-tropical part of the world.

edge – A wine with edge is one with evident (although not excessive) acidity.

élevé – 'Brought up' in French. Much used on wine labels where the wine has been matured (brought up) in oak barrels, *élevé en fûts de chêne*, to give it extra dimensions.

Entre Deux Mers – Meaning 'between two seas', it's a region lying between the Dordogne and Garonne rivers of Bordeaux, now mainly known for dry white wines from Sauvignon and Semillon grapes. Quality rarely seems exciting.

Estremadura – Wine-producing region occupying Portugal's coastal area north of Lisbon. Lots of interesting wines from indigenous grape varieties, usually at bargain prices. If a label mentions Estremadura, it is a safe rule that there might be something good within.

F

Faugères – AC of the Languedoc in south-west France. Source of many hearty, economic reds.

Feteasca – White grape variety widely grown in Romania. Name means 'maiden's grape' and the wine tends to be soft and slightly sweet.

Fiano – White grape variety of Sicily, lately revived. It is said to have been cultivated by the ancient Romans for a wine called Apianum.

finish – The last flavour lingering in the mouth after wine has been swallowed.

fino – Pale and very dry style of sherry. You drink it thoroughly chilled – and you don't keep it any longer after opening than other dry white wines. Needs to be fresh to be at its best.

Fitou – One of the first 'designer' wines, it's an appellation in France's Languedoc region, where production is dominated by one huge co-operative, the Vignerons de Mont Tauch. Back in the 1970s, this co-op paid a corporate-image company to come up with a Fitou logo and label-design style, and the wines have prospered ever since. And it's not just packaging – Fitou at all price levels can be very good value, especially from the Mont Tauch co-op.

flabby – Fun word describing a wine that tastes dilute or watery, with insufficient acidity.

fruit – In tasting terms, the fruit is the greater part of the overall flavour of a wine. The wine is (or should be) after all, composed entirely of fruit.

G

Gamay – The black grape that makes all red Beaujolais and some ordinary burgundy. It is a pretty safe rule to avoid Gamay wines from any other region, but there are exceptions.

Garganega – White grape variety of the Veneto region of north-west Italy. Best known as the principal ingredient of Soave, but occasionally included in varietal blends and mentioned as such on labels. Correctly pronounced 'gar-GAN-iga'.

Garnacha – Spanish black grape variety synonymous with Grenache of France. It is blended with Tempranillo to make the red wines of Rioja and Navarra, and is now quite widely cultivated elsewhere in Spain to make grippingly fruity varietals.

garrigue – Arid land of France's deep south giving its name to a style of red wine that notionally evokes the herby, heated, peppery flavours associated with such a landscape. A tricky metaphor!

Gavi – DOCG for dry but rich white wine from Cortese grapes in Piedmont, north-east Italy. Trendy Gavi di Gavi wines tend to be enjoyably lush, but are rather expensive.

Gewürztraminer – One of the great grape varieties of Alsace, France. At their best, the wines are perfumed with lychees and are richly, spicily fruity, yet quite dry. Gewürztraminer from Alsace is almost always relatively expensive, but the grape is also grown with some success in Eastern Europe, Germany, Italy and South America, and sold at more approachable prices. Pronounced 'ge-VOORTS-traminner'.

Givry – AC for red and white wines in the Côte Chalonnaise sub-region of Burgundy. Source of some wonderfully natural-tasting reds that might be lighter than those of the more prestigious Côte d'Or to the north, but have great merits of their own. Relatively, the wines are often underpriced.

Graciano – Black grape variety of Spain that is one of the minor constituents of Rioja. Better known in its own right in Australia where it can make dense, spicy, long-lived red wines.

green – I don't often use this in the pejorative. Green, to me, is a likeable degree of freshness, especially in Sauvignon Blanc wines.

Grenache – The mainstay of the wines of the southern Rhône Valley in France. Grenache is usually the greater part of the mix in Côtes du Rhône reds and is widely planted right across the neighbouring Languedoc-Roussillon region. It's a big-cropping variety that thrives even in the hottest climates and is really a blending grape – most commonly with Syrah, the noble variety of the northern Rhône. Few French wines are labelled with its name, but the grape has caught on in Australia in a big way and it is now becoming a familiar varietal, known for strong, dark liquorous reds. Grenache is the French name for what is originally a Spanish variety, Garnacha.

Grillo – White grape of Sicily said to be among the island's oldest indigenous varieties, pre-dating the arrival of the Greeks in 600 BC. Much used for fortified Marsala, it has lately been revived for interesting, aromatic dry table wines.

grip – In wine-tasting terminology, the sensation in the mouth produced by a wine that has a healthy quantity of tannin in it. A wine with grip is a good wine. A wine with too much tannin, or which is still too young (the tannin hasn't 'softened' with age) is not described as having grip, but as mouth-puckering – or simply undrinkable.

Grolleau – Black grape variety of the Loire Valley principally cultivated for Rosé d'Anjou.

Grüner Veltliner – The 'national' white-wine grape of Austria. In the past it made mostly soft, German-style everyday wines, but now is behind some excellent dry styles, too.

H

halbtrocken – 'Half-dry' in Germany's wine vocabulary. A reassurance that the wine is not some ghastly sugared Liebfraumilch-style confection.

hock – The wine of Germany's Rhine river valleys. Traditionally, but no longer consistently, it comes in brown bottles, as distinct from the wine of the Mosel river valleys – which comes in green ones.

I

Indicazione Geografica Tipica – Italy's recently instituted wine-quality designation, broadly equivalent to France's vin de pays. The label has to state the geographical location of the vineyard and will often (but not always) state the principal grape varieties from which the wine is made.

J

jammy – the 'sweetness' in dry red wines is supposed to evoke ripeness rather than sugariness. Sometimes, flavours include a sweetness reminiscent of jam. Usually a fault in the winemaking technique.

joven – Young wine, Spanish. In regions such as Rioja, vino joven is a synonym for sin crianza, which means 'without ageing' in cask or bottle.

K

Kabinett – Under Germany's bewildering wine-quality rules, this is a classification of a top-quality (QmP) wine. Expect a keen, dry, racy style. The name comes from the cabinet or cupboard in which winemakers traditionally kept their most treasured bottles.

Kekfrankos – Black grape variety of Hungary, particularly the Sopron region, which makes some of the country's more interesting red wines, characterised by colour and spiciness. Same variety as Austria's Blaufrankisch.

L

Ladoix – Unfashionable AC at northern edge of Côtes de Beaune makes some of Burgundy's true bargain reds. A name to look out for.

Lambrusco – The name is that of a black grape variety widely grown across northern Italy. True Lambrusco wine is red, dry and very slightly sparkling, but from the 1980s Britain has been deluged with a strange, sweet manifestation of the style, which has done little to enhance the good name of the original. Good Lambrusco is delicious and fun, but in this country now very hard to find. See section for Booths.

Languedoc-Roussillon – Vast area of southern France, including the country's south-west Mediterranean region. The source, now, of many great-value wines from countless ACs and vin de pays zones.

legs – The liquid residue left clinging to the sides of the glass after wine has been swirled. The persistence of the legs is an indicator of the weight of alcohol. Also known as 'tears'.

lieu dit – This is starting to appear on French wine labels. It translates as an 'agreed place' and is an area of vineyard defined as of particular character or merit, but not classified under wine law. Usually, the lieu dit's name is stated, with the implication that the wine in question has special value.

liquorice – The pungent slightly burnt flavours of this once-fashionable confection are detectable in some wines made from very ripe grapes, for example, the Malbec harvested in Argentina and several varieties grown in the very hot vineyards of southernmost Italy. A close synonym is 'tarry'. This characteristic is by no means a fault in red wine, unless very dominant, but it can make for a challenging flavour that might not appeal to all tastes.

liquorous – Wines of great weight and glyceriney texture (evidenced by the 'legs', or 'tears', which cling to the glass after the wine has been swirled) are always noteworthy. The connection with liquor is drawn in respect of the feel of the wine in the mouth, rather than with the higher alcoholic strength of spirits.

Lugana – DOC of Lombardy, Italy known for a dry white wine that is often of real distinction – rich, almondy stuff from the ubiquitous Trebbiano grape.

M

Macabeo – One of the main grapes used for cava, the sparkling wine of Spain. It is the same grape as Viura.

Mâcon – Town and collective appellation of southern Burgundy, France. Lightweight white wines from Chardonnay grapes and similarly light reds from Pinot Noir and some Gamay. The better ones, and the ones exported, have the AC Mâcon-Villages and there are individual-village wines with their own ACs including Mâcon-Clessé, Mâcon-Viré and Mâcon-Lugny.

Malbec – Black grape variety grown on a small scale in Bordeaux, and the mainstay of the wines of Cahors in France's Dordogne region under the name Cot. Now much better known for producing big butch reds in Argentina.

Manzanilla – Pale, very dry sherry of Sanlucar de Barrameda, a resort town on the Bay of Cadiz in Spain. Manzanilla is proud to be distinct from the pale, very dry fino sherry of the main producing town of Jerez de la Frontera an hour's drive inland. Drink it chilled and fresh – it goes downhill in an opened bottle after just a few days, even if kept (as it should be) in the fridge.

Margaret River – Vineyard region of Western Australia regarded as ideal for grape varieties including Cabernet Sauvignon. It has a relatively cool climate and a reputation for making sophisticated wines, both red and white.

Marlborough – Best-known vineyard region of New Zealand's South Island has a cool climate and a name for brisk but cerebral Sauvignon Blanc and Chardonnay wines.

Marsanne – White grape variety of the northern Rhône Valley and, increasingly, of the wider south of France. It's known for making well-coloured wines with heady aroma and fruit.

Mataro – Black grape variety of Australia. It's the same as the Mourvèdre of France and Monastrell of Spain.

McLaren Vale – Vineyard region south of Adelaide in south-east Australia. Known for blockbuster Shiraz (and Chardonnay) that can be of great balance and quality from winemakers who keep the ripeness under control.

meaty – Weighty, rich red wine style.

Mendoza – The region to watch in Argentina. Lying to the east of the Andes mountains, just about opposite the best vineyards of Chile on the other side, Mendoza accounts for the bulk of Argentine wine production, with quality improving fast.

Merlot – One of the great black wine grapes of Bordeaux, and now grown all over the world. The name is said to derive from the French merle, meaning a blackbird. Characteristics of Merlot-based wines attract descriptions such as 'plummy' and 'plump' with black-cherry aroma. The grapes are larger than most, and thus have less skin in proportion to their flesh. This means the resulting wines have less tannin than wines from smaller-berry varieties such as Cabernet Sauvignon, and are therefore, in the Bordeaux context at least, more suitable for drinking while still relatively young.

middle palate – In wine-tasting, the impression given by the wine when it is held in the mouth.

Midi – Catch-all term for the deep south of France west of the Rhône Valley.

mineral – Good dry white wines can have a crispness and freshness that somehow evokes this word. Purity of flavour is a key.

Minervois – AC for (mostly) red wines from vineyards around the town of Minerve in the Languedoc-Roussillon region of France. Often good value. The new Minervois La Livinière AC – a sort of Minervois Grand Cru – is host to some great estates including Château Maris and Vignobles Lorgeril.

Monastrell – Black grape variety of Spain, widely planted in Mediterranean regions for inexpensive wines notable for their high alcohol and toughness – though they can mature into excellent, soft reds. The variety is known in France as Mourvèdre and in Australia as Mataro.

Monbazillac – AC for sweet, dessert wines within the wider appellation of Bergerac in south-west France. Made from the same grape varieties (principally Sauvignon and Semillon) that go into the much costlier counterpart wines of Barsac and Sauternes near Bordeaux, these stickies from botrytis-affected, late-harvested grapes can be delicious and good value for money.

Montalcino – Hill town of Tuscany, Italy, and a DOCG for strong and very long-lived red wines from Brunello grapes. The wines are mostly very expensive. Rosso di Montalcino, a DOC for the humbler wines of the zone, is often a good buy.

Montepulciano – Black grape variety of Italy. Best known in Montepulciano d'Abruzzo, the juicy, purply-black and bramble-fruited red of the Abruzzi region midway down Italy's Adriatic side. Also the grape in the rightly popular hearty reds of Rosso Conero from around Ancona in the Marches. Not to be confused with the hill town of Montepulciano in Tuscany, famous for expensive Vino Nobile di Montepulciano wine.

morello – Lots of red wines have smells and flavours redolent of cherries. Morello cherries, among the darkest coloured and sweetest of all varieties and the preferred choice of cherry-brandy producers, have a distinct sweetness resembled by some wines made from Merlot grapes. A morello whiff or taste is generally very welcome.

Moscatel – Spanish Muscat.

Moscato – *See* Muscat.

Moselle – The wine of Germany's Mosel river valleys, collectively known for winemaking purposes as Mosel-Saar-Ruwer. The wine always comes in slim, green bottles, as distinct from the brown bottles traditionally employed for Rhine wines.

Mourvèdre – Widely planted black grape variety of southern France. It's an ingredient in many of the wines of Provence, the Rhône and Languedoc, including the ubiquitous vin de pays d'Oc. It's a hot-climate vine and the wine is usually blended with other varieties to give sweet aromas and 'backbone' to the mix. Known as Mataro in Australia and Monastrell in Spain.

Muscadet – One of France's most familiar everyday whites, made from a grape called the Melon or Melon de Bourgogne. It comes from vineyards at the estuarial end of the River Loire, and has a sea-breezy freshness about it. The better wines are reckoned to be those from the vineyards in the Sèvre et Maine region, and many are made sur lie – 'on the lees' – meaning that the wine is left in contact with the yeasty deposit of its fermentation until just before bottling, in an endeavour to add interest to what can sometimes be an acidic and fruitless style.

Muscat – Grape variety with origins in ancient Greece, and still grown widely among the Aegean islands for the production of sweet white wines. Muscats are the wines that taste more like grape juice than any other – but the high sugar levels ensure they are also among the most alcoholic of wines, too. Known as Moscato in Italy, the grape is much used for making sweet sparkling wines, as in Asti Spumante or Moscato d'Asti. There are several appellations in south-west France for inexpensive Muscats made rather like port, part-fermented before the addition of grape alcohol to halt the conversion of sugar into alcohol, creating a sweet and heady vin doux naturel. Dry Muscat wines, when well made, have a delicious sweet aroma but a refreshing, light touch with flavours reminiscent variously of orange blossom, wood smoke and grapefruit.

must – New-pressed grape juice prior to fermentation.

N

Navarra – DO wine-producing region of northern Spain adjacent to, and overshadowed by, Rioja. Navarra's wines can be startlingly akin to their neighbouring rivals, and sometimes rather better value for money.

négociant – In France, a dealer-producer who buys wines from growers and matures and/or blends them for sale under his own label. Purists can be a bit sniffy about these entrepreneurs, claiming that only the vine-grower with his or her own winemaking set-up can make truly authentic stuff, but the truth is that many of the best wines of France are négociant-produced – especially at the humbler end of the price scale. Négociants are often identified on wine labels as négociant-éleveur (literally 'dealer-bringer-up') and meaning that the wine has been matured, blended and bottled by the party in question.

Negroamaro – Black grape variety mainly of Apulia, the fast-improving wine region of south-east Italy. Dense, earthy red wines with ageing potential and plenty of alcohol. The grape behind Copertino.

Nerello Mascalese – Black grape of Sicily making light, flavoursome and alcoholic reds.

Nero d'Avola – Black grape variety of Sicily and southern Italy. It makes deep-coloured wines that, given half a chance, can develop intensity and richness with age.

non-vintage – A wine is described as such when it has been blended from the harvests of more than one year. A non-vintage wine is not necessarily an inferior one, but under quality-control regulations around the world, still table wines most usually derive solely from one year's grape crop to qualify for appellation status. Champagnes and sparkling wines are mostly blended from several vintages, as are fortified wines, such as basic port and sherry.

nose – In the vocabulary of the wine-taster, the nose is the scent of a wine. Sounds a bit dotty, but it makes a sensible enough alternative to the rather bald 'smell'. The use of the word 'perfume' implies that the wine smells particularly good. 'Aroma' is used specifically to describe a wine that smells as it should, as in 'this burgundy has the authentic strawberry-raspberry aroma of Pinot Noir'.

O

oak – Most of the world's most expensive wines are matured in new or nearly new oak barrels, giving additional opulence of flavour. Of late, many cheaper wines have been getting the oak treatment, too, in older, cheaper casks, or simply by having sacks of oak chippings poured into their steel or fibreglass holding tanks. 'Oak aged' on a label is likely to indicate the latter treatments. But the overtly oaked wines of Australia have in some cases been so overdone that there is now a reactive trend whereby some producers proclaim their wines – particularly Chardonnays – as 'unoaked' on the label, thereby asserting that the flavours are more naturally achieved.

Oltrepo Pavese – Wine-producing zone of Piedmont, north-west Italy. The name means 'south of Pavia across the [river] Po' and the wines, both white and red, can be excellent quality and value for money.

organic wine – As in other sectors of the food industry, demand for organically made wine is – or appears to be – growing. As a rule, a wine qualifies as organic if it comes entirely from grapes grown in vineyards cultivated without the use of synthetic materials, and made in a winery where chemical treatments or additives are shunned with similar vigour. In fact, there are plenty of winemakers in the world using organic methods, but who disdain to label their bottles as such. Wines proclaiming their organic status used to carry the same sort of premium as their counterparts round the corner in the fruit, vegetable and meat aisles. But organic viticulture is now commonplace and there seems little price impact. There is no single worldwide (or even Europe-wide) standard for organic food or wine, so you pretty much have to take the producer's word for it.

P

Pasqua – One of the biggest and, it should be said, best wine producers of the Veneto region of north-west Italy.

Passetoutgrains – Bourgogne passetoutgrains is a generic appellation of the Burgundy region, France. The word loosely means 'any grapes allowed' and is supposed specifically to designate a red wine made with Gamay grapes as well as Burgundy's principal black variety, Pinot Noir, in a ratio of two parts Gamay to one of Pinot. The wine is usually relatively inexpensive, and relatively uninteresting, too.

Periquita – Black grape variety of southern Portugal. Makes rather exotic spicy reds. Name means 'parrot'.

Petit Verdot – Black grape variety of Bordeaux used to give additional colour, density and spiciness to Cabernet Sauvignon-dominated blends. Mostly a minority player at home, but in Australia and California it is grown as the principal variety for some big hearty reds of real character.

petrol – When white wines from certain grapes, especially Riesling, are allowed to age in the bottle for longer than a year or two, they can take on a spirity aroma reminiscent of petrol or diesel. In grand mature German wines, this is considered a very good thing.

Picpoul – Grape variety of southern France. Best known in Picpoul de Pinet, a dry white from near Carcassonne in the Languedoc. The name Picpoul means 'stings the lips' – referring to the natural high acidity of the juice.

Piemonte – North-western province of Italy, which we call Piedmont, known for the spumante wines of the town of Asti, plus expensive Barbaresco and Barolo and better-value varietal red wines from Barbera and Dolcetto grapes.

Pinotage – South Africa's own black grape variety. Makes red wines ranging from light and juicy to dark, strong and long-lived. It's a cross between Pinot Noir and a grape the South Africans used to call Hermitage (thus the portmanteau name) but turns out to have been Cinsault.

Pinot Blanc – White grape variety principally of Alsace, France. Florally perfumed, exotically fruity dry white wines.

Pinot Grigio – White grape variety of northern Italy. Wines bearing its name are perplexingly fashionable. Good examples have an interesting smoky-pungent aroma and keen, slaking fruit. But most are dull. Originally French, it is at its best in the lushly exotic Pinot Gris wines of Alsace.

Pinot Noir – The great black grape of Burgundy, France. It makes all the region's fabulously expensive red wines. Notoriously difficult to grow in warmer climates, it is nevertheless cultivated by countless intrepid winemakers in the New World intent on reproducing the magic appeal of red burgundy. California and New Zealand have come closest, but rarely at prices much below those for the real thing. Some Chilean Pinot Noirs are inexpensive and worth trying.

Pouilly Fuissé – Village and AC of the Mâconnais region of southern Burgundy in France. Dry white wines from Chardonnay grapes. Wines are among the highest rated of the Mâconnais.

Pouilly Fumé – Village and AC of the Loire Valley in France. Dry white wines from Sauvignon Blanc grapes. Similar 'pebbly', 'grassy' or even 'gooseberry' style to neighbouring AC Sancerre. The notion put about by some enthusiasts that Pouilly Fumé is 'smoky' is surely nothing more than word association with the name.

Primitivo – Black grape variety of southern Italy, especially the region of Puglia. Named from Latin *primus* for first, the grape is among the earliest-ripening of all varieties. The wines are typically dense and dark in colour with plenty of alcohol, and have an earthy, spicy style. Often a real bargain.

Prosecco – White grape variety of Italy's Veneto region known entirely for the softly sparkling wine it makes. The best come from the DOC Conegliano-Valdobbiadene, made as spumante ('foaming') wines in pressurised tanks, typically to 11 per cent alcohol and ranging from softly sweet to crisply dry. Now trendy, but the cheap wines – one leading brand comes in a can – are of very variable quality.

Puglia – The region occupying the 'heel' of southern Italy, lately making many good, inexpensive wines from indigenous grape varieties.

Q

QbA – German, standing for Qualitätswein bestimmter Anbaugebiete. It means 'quality wine from designated areas' and implies that the wine is made from grapes with a minimum level of ripeness, but it's by no means a guarantee of exciting quality. Only wines labelled QmP (see next entry) can be depended upon to be special.

QmP – Stands for Qualitätswein mit Prädikat. These are the serious wines of Germany, made without the addition of sugar to 'improve' them. To qualify for QmP status, the grapes must reach a level of ripeness as measured on a sweetness scale – all according to Germany's fiendishly complicated wine-quality regulations. Wines from grapes that reach the stated minimum level of sweetness qualify for the description of Kabinett. The next level up earns the rank of Spätlese, meaning 'late-picked'. Kabinett wines can be expected to be dry and brisk in style, and Spätlese wines a little bit riper and fuller. The next grade up, Auslese, meaning 'selected harvest', indicates a wine made from super-ripe grapes; it will be golden in colour and honeyed in flavour. A generation ago, these wines were as valued, and as expensive, as any of the world's grandest appellations, but the collapse in demand for German wines in the UK – brought about by the disrepute rightly earned for floods of filthy Liebfraumilch – means they are now seriously undervalued.

Quincy – AC of Loire Valley, France, known for pebbly-dry white wines from Sauvignon grapes. The wines are forever compared to those of nearby and much better-known Sancerre – and Quincy often represents better value for money. Pronounced 'KAN-see'.

Quinta – Portuguese for farm or estate. It precedes the names of many of Portugal's best-known wines. It is pronounced 'KEEN-ta'.

R

racy – Evocative wine-tasting description for wine that thrills the tastebuds with a rush of exciting sensations. Good Rieslings often qualify.

raisiny – Wines from grapes that have been very ripe or overripe at harvest can take on a smell and flavour akin to the concentrated, heat-dried sweetness of raisins. As a minor element in the character of a wine, this can add to the appeal but as a dominant characteristic it is a fault.

rancio – Spanish term harking back to Roman times when wines were commonly stored in jars outside, exposed to the sun, so they oxidised and took on a burnt sort of flavour. Today, rancio describes a baked – and by no means unpleasant – flavour in fortified wines, particularly sherry and Madeira.

Reserva – In Portugal and Spain, this has genuine significance. The Portuguese use it for special wines with a higher alcohol level and longer ageing, although the precise periods vary between regions. In Spain, especially in the Navarra and Rioja regions, it means the wine must have had at least a year in oak and two in bottle before release.

reserve – On French (as réserve) or other wines, this implies special-quality, longer-aged wines, but has no official significance.

Retsina – The universal white wine of Greece. It has been traditionally made in Attica, the region of Athens, for a very long time, and is said to owe its origins and name to the ancient custom of sealing amphorae (terracotta jars) of the wine with a gum made from pine resin. Some of the flavour of the resin inevitably transmitted itself into the wine, and ancient Greeks acquired a lasting taste for it.

Reuilly – AC of Loire Valley, France, for crisp dry whites from Sauvignon grapes. Pronounced 'RER-yee'.

Ribatejo – Emerging wine region of Portugal. Worth seeking out on labels of red wines in particular, because new winemakers are producing lively stuff from distinctive indigenous grapes such as Castelao and Trincadeira.

Ribera del Duero – Classic wine region of north-west Spain lying along the River Duero (which crosses the border to become Portugal's Douro, forming the valley where port comes from). It is the home to an estate rather oddly named Vega Sicilia, where red wines of epic quality are made and sold at equally epic prices. Further down the scale, some very good reds are made, too.

Riesling – The noble grape variety of Germany. It is correctly pronounced 'REEZ-ling', not 'RICE-ling'. Once notorious as the grape behind all those boring 'medium' Liebfraumilches and Niersteiners, this grape has had a bad press. In fact, there has never been much, if any, Riesling in Germany's cheap-and-nasty plonks. But the country's best wines, the so-called Qualitätswein mit Prädikat grades, are made almost exclusively with Riesling. These wines range from crisply fresh and appley styles to extravagantly fruity, honeyed wines from late-harvested grapes. Excellent Riesling wines are also made in Alsace and now in Australia.

Rioja – The principal fine-wine region of Spain, in the country's north east. The pricier wines are noted for their vanilla-pod richness from long ageing in oak casks. Tempranillo and Garnacha grapes make the reds, Viura the whites.

Ripasso – A particular style of Valpolicella wine. New wine is partially refermented in vats that have been used to make the recioto reds (wines made from semi-dried grapes), thus creating a bigger, smoother version of usually light and pale Valpolicella.

Riserva – In Italy, a wine made only in the best vintages, and allowed longer ageing in cask and bottle.

Rivaner – Alternative name for Germany's Müller-Thurgau grape, the life-blood of Liebfraumilch.

Riverland – Vineyard region to the immediate north of the Barossa Valley of South Australia, extending east into New South Wales.

Roditis – White grape variety of Greece, known for fresh dry whites with decent acidity, often included in retsina.

rosso – Red wine, Italy.

Rosso Conero – DOC red wine made in the environs of Ancona in the Marches, Italy. Made from the Montepulciano grape, the wine can provide excellent value for money.

Ruby Cabernet – Black grape variety of California, created by crossing Cabernet Sauvignon and Carignan. Makes soft and squelchy red wine at home and in South Africa.

Rueda – DO of north-west Spain making first-class refreshing dry whites from the indigenous Verdejo grape, imported Sauvignon, and others. Exciting quality, and prices are keen.

Rully – AC of Chalonnais region of southern Burgundy, France. White wines from Chardonnay and red wines from Pinot Noir grapes. Both can be very good and are substantially cheaper than their more northerly Burgundian neighbours. Pronounced 'ROO-yee'.

S

Saint Emilion – AC of Bordeaux, France. Centred on the romantic hill town of St Emilion, this famous sub-region makes some of the grandest red wines of France, but also some of the best-value ones. Less fashionable than the Médoc region on the opposite (west) bank of the River Gironde that bisects Bordeaux, St Emilion wines are made largely with the Merlot grape, and are relatively quick to mature. The grandest wines are classified 1er grand cru classé and are madly expensive, but many more are classified respectively grand cru classé and grand cru, and these designations can be seen as a fairly trustworthy indicator of quality. There are several 'satellite' St Emilion ACs named after the villages at their centres, notably Lussac St Emilion, Montagne St Emilion and Puisseguin St Emilion. Some excellent wines are made by estates within these ACs, and at relatively affordable prices thanks to the comparatively humble status of their satellite designations.

Salento – Up-and-coming wine region of southern Italy. Many good bargain reds from local grapes including Nero d'Avola and Primitivo.

Sancerre – AC of the Loire Valley, France, renowned for flinty-fresh Sauvignon whites and rarer Pinot Noir reds. These wines are never cheap, and recent tastings make it plain that only the best-made, individual-producer wines are worth the money. Budget brands seem mostly dull.

Sangiovese – The local black grape of Tuscany, Italy. It is the principal variety used for Chianti and is now widely planted in Latin America – often making delicious, Chianti-like wines with characteristic cherryish-but-deeply-ripe fruit and a dry, clean finish. Chianti wines have become (unjustifiably) expensive in recent years and cheaper Italian wines such as those called Sangiovese di Toscana make a consoling substitute.

Saumur – Town and appellation of Loire Valley, France. Characterful minerally red wines from Cabernet Franc grapes, and some whites. The once-popular sparkling wines from Chenin Blanc grapes are now little seen in Britain.

Saumur-Champigny – Separate appellation for red wines from Cabernet Franc grapes of Saumur in the Loire, sometimes very good and lively.

Sauvignon Blanc – French white grape variety now grown worldwide. New Zealand is successfully challenging the long supremacy of French ACs such as Sancerre. The wines are characterised by aromas of gooseberry, fresh-cut grass, even asparagus. Flavours are often described as 'grassy' or 'nettly'.

sec – Dry wine style. French.

secco – Dry wine style. Italian.

Semillon – White grape variety originally of Bordeaux, where it is blended with Sauvignon Blanc to make fresh dry whites and, when harvested very late in the season, the ambrosial sweet whites of Barsac, Sauternes and other appellations. Even in the driest wines, the grape can be recognised from its honeyed, sweet-pineapple, even banana-like aromas. Now widely planted in Australia and Latin America, and frequently blended with Chardonnay to make dry whites, some of them interesting.

sherry – The great aperitif wine of Spain, centred on the Andalusian city of Jerez (from which the name 'sherry' is an English mispronunciation). There is a lot of sherry-style wine in the world, but only the authentic wine from Jerez and the neighbouring producing towns of Puerta de Santa Maria and Sanlucar de Barrameda may label their wines as such. The Spanish drink real sherry – very dry and fresh, pale in colour and served well-chilled – called fino and manzanilla, and darker but naturally dry variations called amontillado, palo cortado and oloroso.

Shiraz – Australian name for the Syrah grape. The variety is the most widely planted of any in Australia, and makes red wines of wildly varying quality, characterised by dense colour, high alcohol, spicy fruit and generous, cushiony texture.

Somontano – Wine region of north-east Spain. Name means 'under the mountains' – in this case the Pyrenees – and the region has had DO status since 1984. Much innovative winemaking here, with New

World styles emerging. Some very good buys. A region to watch.

souple – French wine-tasting term that translates into English as 'supple' or even 'docile' as in 'pliable', but I understand it in the vinous context to mean muscular but soft – a wine with tannin as well as soft fruit.

Spätlese – *See* QmP.

spirity – Some wines, mostly from the New World, are made from grapes so ripe at harvest that their high alcohol content can be detected through a mildly burning sensation on the tongue, similar to the effect of sipping a spirit.

spritzy – Describes a wine with a barely detectable sparkle. Some young wines are intended to have this elusive fizziness; in others it is a fault.

spumante – Sparkling wine of Italy. Asti Spumante is the best known, from the town of Asti in the north-west Italian province of Piemonte. The term describes wines that are fully sparkling. Frizzante wines have a less vigorous mousse.

stalky – A useful tasting term to describe red wines with flavours that make you think the stalks from the grape bunches must have been fermented along with the must (juice). Young Bordeaux reds very often have this mild astringency. In moderation it's fine, but if it dominates it probably signifies the wine is at best immature and at worst badly made.

Stellenbosch – Town and region at the heart of South Africa's burgeoning wine industry. It's an hour's drive from Cape Town and the source of much of the country's cheaper wine. Quality is variable, and the name Stellenbosch on a label can't (yet, anyway) be taken as a guarantee of quality.

stony – Wine-tasting term for keenly dry white wines. It's meant to indicate a wine of purity and real quality, with just the right match of fruit and acidity.

structured – Good wines are not one-dimensional, they have layers of flavour and texture. A structured wine has phases of enjoyment: the 'attack', or first impression in the mouth; the middle palate as the wine is held in the mouth; and the lingering aftertaste.

summer fruit – Wine-tasting term intended to convey a smell or taste of soft fruits such as strawberries and raspberries – without having to commit too specifically to which.

Superiore – On labels of Italian wines, this is more than an idle boast. Under DOC rules, wines must qualify for the superiore designation by reaching one or more specified quality levels, usually a higher alcohol content or an additional period of maturation. Frascati, for example, qualifies for DOC status at 11.5 per cent alcohol, but to be classified superiore must have 12 per cent alcohol.

sur lie – Literally, 'on the lees'. It's a term now widely used on the labels of Muscadet wines, signifying that after fermentation has died down, the new wine has been left in the tank over the winter on the lees – the detritus of yeasts and other interesting compounds left over from the turbid fermentation process. The idea is that additional interest is imparted into the flavour of the wine.

Syrah – The noble grape of the Rhône Valley, France. Makes very dark, dense wine characterised by peppery, tarry aromas. Now planted all over southern France and farther afield. In Australia, where it makes wines ranging from disagreeably jam-like plonks to wonderfully rich and silky keeping wines, it is known as Shiraz.

T

table wine – Wine that is unfortified and of an alcoholic strength, for UK tax purposes anyway, of no more than 15 per cent. I use the term to distinguish, for example, between the red table wines of the Douro Valley in Portugal and the region's better-known fortified wine, port.

Tafelwein – Table wine, German. The humblest quality designation, which doesn't usually bode very well.

tank method – Bulk-production process for sparkling wines. Base wine undergoes secondary fermentation in a large, sealed vat rather than in individual closed bottles. Also known as the Charmat method after the name of the inventor of the process.

Tannat – Black grape of south-west France, notably for wines of Madiran, and lately named as the variety most beneficial to health thanks to its outstanding antioxidant content.

tannin – Well known as the film-forming, teeth-coating component in tea, tannin is a natural compound that occurs in black grape skins and acts as a natural preservative in wine. Its noticeable presence in wine is regarded as a good thing. It gives young everyday reds their dryness, firmness of flavour and backbone. And it helps high-quality reds to retain their lively fruitiness for many years. A grand Bordeaux red when first made, for example, will have purply-sweet, rich fruit and mouth-puckering tannin, but after ten years or so this will have evolved into a delectably fruity, mature wine in which the formerly parching effects of the tannin have receded almost completely, leaving the shade of 'residual tannin' that marks out a great wine approaching maturity.

Tarrango – Black grape variety of Australia.

tarry – On the whole, winemakers don't like critics to say their wines evoke the redolence of road repairs, but I can't help using this term to describe the agreeable, sweet, 'burnt' flavour that is often found at the centre of the fruit in wines from Argentina, Italy and Portugal in particular.

TCA – Dreaded ailment in wine, usually blamed on faulty corks. It stands for 246 *trichloroanisol* and is characterised by a horrible musty smell and flavour in the affected wine. It is largely because of the current plague of TCA that so many wine producers worldwide are now going over to polymer 'corks' and screwcaps.

tears – The colourless alcohol in the wine left clinging to the inside of the glass after the contents have been swirled. Persistent tears (also known as 'legs') indicate a wine of good concentration.

Tempranillo – The great black grape of Spain. Along with Garnacha (Grenache in France) it makes all red Rioja and Navarra wines and, under many pseudonyms, is an important or exclusive contributor to the wines of many other regions of Spain. It is also widely cultivated in South America.

tinto – On Spanish labels indicates a deeply coloured red wine. Clarete denotes a paler colour. Also Portuguese.

Toro – Quality wine region east of Zamora, Spain.

Torrontes – White grape variety of Argentina. Makes soft, dry wines often with delicious grapy-spicy aroma, similar in style to the classic dry Muscat wines of Alsace, but at more accessible prices.

Touraine – Region encompassing a swathe of the Loire Valley, France. Non-AC wines may be labelled 'Sauvignon de Touraine' etc.

Touriga Nacional – The most valued black grape variety of the Douro Valley in Portugal, where port is made. The name Touriga now appears on an increasing number of table wines made as sidelines by the port producers. They can be very good, with the same spirity aroma and sleek flavours of port itself, minus the fortification.

Traminer – Grape variety, the same as Gewürztraminer.

Trebbiano – The workhorse white grape of Italy. A productive variety that is easy to cultivate, it seems to be included in just about every ordinary white wine of the entire nation – including Frascati, Orvieto and Soave. It is the same grape as France's Ugni Blanc. There are, however, distinct regional variations of the grape. Trebbiano di Lugana makes a distinctive white in the DOC of the name, sometimes very good, while Trebbiano di Toscana makes a major contribution to the distinctly less interesting dry whites of Chianti country.

Trincadeira Preta – Portuguese black grape variety native to the port-producing vineyards of the Douro Valley (where it goes under the name Tinta Amarella). In southern Portugal, it produces dark and sturdy table wines.

trocken – 'Dry' German wine. It's a recent trend among commercial-scale producers in the Rhine and Mosel to label their wines with this description in the hope of reassuring consumers that the contents do not resemble the dreaded sugar-water Liebfraumilch-type plonks of the bad old days. But the description does have a particular meaning under German wine law, namely that there is only a low level of unfermented sugar lingering in the wine (9 grams per litre, if you need to know), and this can leave the wine tasting rather austere.

U

Ugni Blanc – The most widely cultivated white grape variety of France and the mainstay of many a cheap dry white wine. To date it has been better known as the provider of base wine for distilling into armagnac and cognac, but lately the name has been appearing on wine labels. Technology seems to be improving the performance of the grape. The curious name is pronounced 'OON-yee', and is the same variety as Italy's ubiquitous Trebbiano.

V

Vacqueyras – Village of the southern Rhône Valley of France in the region better known for its generic appellation, the Côtes du Rhône. Vacqueyras can date its winemaking history all the way back to 1414, but has only been producing under its own village AC since 1991. The wines, from Grenache and Syrah grapes, can be wonderfully silky and intense, spicy and long-lived.

Valdepeñas – An island of quality production amidst the ocean of mediocrity that is Spain's La Mancha region – where most of the grapes are grown for distilling into the head-banging brandies of Jerez. Valdepeñas reds are made from a grape they call the Cencibel – which turns out to be a very close relation of the Tempranillo grape that is the mainstay of the fine but expensive red wines of Rioja. Again, like Rioja, Valdepeñas wines are matured in oak casks to give them a vanilla-rich smoothness. Among bargain reds, Valdepeñas is a name to look out for.

Valpolicella – Red wine of Verona, Italy. Good examples have ripe, cherry fruit and a pleasingly dry finish. Unfortunately, there are many bad examples of Valpolicella. Shop with circumspection. Valpolicella Classico wines, from the best vineyards clustered around the town, are more reliable. Those additionally labelled Superiore have higher alcohol and some bottle age.

vanilla – Ageing wines in oak barrels (or, less picturesquely, adding oak chips to wine in huge concrete vats) imparts a range of characteristics including a smell of vanilla from the ethyl vanilline naturally given off by oak.

varietal – A varietal wine is one named after the grape variety (one or more) from which it is made. Nearly all everyday wines worldwide are now labelled in this way. It is salutary to contemplate that just 30 years ago, wines described thus were virtually unknown outside Germany and one or two quirky regions of France and Italy.

vegan-friendly – My informal way of noting that a wine is claimed to have been made not only with animal-product-free finings (*see* Vegetarian wine) but without any animal-related products whatsoever, such as manure in the vineyards.

vegetal – A tasting note definitely open to interpretation. It suggests a smell or flavour reminiscent less of fruit (apple, pineapple, strawberry and the like) than of something leafy or even root based. Some wines are evocative (to some tastes) of beetroot, cabbage or even unlikelier vegetable flavours – and these characteristics may add materially to the attraction of the wine.

vegetarian wine – Wines labelled 'suitable for vegetarians' have been made without the assistance of animal products for 'fining' – clarifying – before bottling. Gelatine, egg whites, isinglass from fish bladders and casein from milk are among the items shunned, usually in favour of bentonite, an absorbent clay first found at Benton in the US state of Montana.

Verdejo – White grape of the Rueda region in north-west Spain. It can make superbly perfumed crisp dry whites of truly distinctive character and has helped make Rueda one of the best white-wine sources of Europe. No relation to Verdelho.

Verdelho – Portuguese grape variety once mainly used for a medium-dry style of Madeira, also called Verdelho, but now rare. The vine is now prospering in Australia, where it can make well-balanced dry whites with fleeting richness and lemon-lime acidity.

Verdicchio – White grape variety of Italy best known in the DOC zone of Castelli dei Jesi in the Adriatic wine region of the Marches. Dry white wines once known for little more than their naff amphora-style bottles but now gaining a reputation for interesting, herbaceous flavours of recognisable character.

Vermentino – White grape variety principally of Italy, especially Sardinia. Makes florally scented soft dry whites.

Vieilles vignes – Old vines. Many French producers like to claim on their labels that the wine within is from vines of notable antiquity. While it's true that vines don't produce useful grapes for the first few years after planting, it is uncertain whether vines of much greater age – say 25 years plus – than others actually make better fruit. There are no regulations governing the use of the term, so it's not a reliable indicator anyway.

Vin Délimité de Qualité Supérieure – Usually abbreviated to VDQS, a French wine-quality designation between appellation contrôlée and vin de pays. To qualify, the wine has to be from approved grape varieties grown in a defined zone. This designation is gradually disappearing.

vin de liqueur – Sweet style of white wine mostly from the Pyrenean region of south-westernmost France, made by adding a little spirit to the new wine before it has fermented out, halting the fermentation and retaining sugar.

vin de pays – 'Country wine' of France. The French map is divided up into more than 100 vin de pays regions. Wine in bottles labelled as such must be from grapes grown in the nominated zone or département. Some vin de pays areas are huge: the Vin de Pays d'Oc (named after the Languedoc region) covers much of the Midi and Provence. Plenty of wines bearing this humble designation are of astoundingly high quality and certainly compete with New World counterparts for interest and value.

Vin de Pays d'Oc – Largest of the zones, encompasses much of the huge region of the Languedoc of south-west France. Many excellent wines are sold under this classification, particularly those made in appellation areas from grapes not permitted locally.

vin de table – The humblest official classification of French wine. Neither the region, grape varieties nor vintage need be stated on the label. The wine might not even be French. Don't expect too much from this kind of 'table wine'.

vin doux naturel – Sweet, mildly fortified wine of southern France. A little spirit is added during the winemaking process, halting the fermentation by killing the yeast before it has consumed all the sugars – hence the pronounced sweetness of the wine.

vin gris – Rosé wine from Provence.

Vinho de mesa – 'Table wine' of Portugal.

Vino da tavola – The humblest official classification of Italian wine. Much ordinary plonk bears this designation, but the bizarre quirks of Italy's wine laws dictate that some of that country's finest wines are also classed as mere vino da tavola (table wine). If an expensive Italian wine is labelled as such, it doesn't mean it will be a disappointment.

Vino de mesa – 'Table wine' of Spain. Usually very ordinary.

vintage – The grape harvest. The year displayed on bottle labels is the year of the harvest. Wines bearing no date have been blended from the harvests of two or more years.

Viognier – A grape variety once exclusive to the northern Rhône Valley in France where it makes a very chi-chi wine, Condrieu, usually costing £20 plus. Now, the Viognier is grown more widely, in North and South America as well as elsewhere in France, and occasionally produces soft, marrowy whites that echo the grand style of Condrieu itself. The Viognier is now commonly blended with Shiraz in red winemaking in Australia and South Africa. It does not dilute the colour and is confidently believed by highly experienced winemakers to enhance the quality. Steve Webber, in charge of winemaking at the revered De Bortoli estates in the Yarra Valley region of Victoria, Australia, puts between two and five per cent Viognier in with some of his Shiraz wines. 'I think it's the perfume,' he told me. 'It gives some femininity to the wine.'

Viura – White grape variety of Rioja, Spain. Also widely grown elsewhere in Spain under the name Macabeo. Wines have a blossomy aroma and are dry, but sometimes soft at the expense of acidity.

Vouvray – AC of the Loire Valley, France, known for still and sparkling dry white wines and sweet, still whites from late-harvested grapes. The wines, all from Chenin Blanc grapes, have a unique capacity for unctuous softness combined with lively freshness – an effect best portrayed in the demi-sec (slightly sweet) wines, which can be delicious and keenly priced. Unfashionable, but worth looking out for.

Vranac – Black grape variety of the Balkans known for dense colour and tangy-bitter edge to the flavour. Best enjoyed in situ.

W

weight – In an ideal world the weight of a wine is determined by the ripeness of the grapes from which it has been made. In some cases the weight is determined merely by the quantity of sugar added during the production process. A good, genuine wine described as having weight is one in which there is plenty of alcohol and 'extract' – colour and flavour from the grapes. Wine enthusiasts judge weight by swirling the wine in the glass and then examining the 'legs' or 'tears' left clinging to the inside of the glass after the contents have subsided. Alcohol gives these runlets a dense, glycerine-like condition, and if they cling for a long time, the wine is deemed to have weight – a very good thing in all honestly made wines.

Winzergenossenschaft – One of the many very lengthy and peculiar words regularly found on labels of German wines. This means a winemaking co-operative. Many excellent German wines are made by these associations of growers.

woodsap – A subjective tasting note. Some wines have a fleeting bitterness, which is not a fault, but an interesting balancing factor amidst very ripe flavours. The effect somehow evokes woodsap.

X

Xarel-lo – One of the main grape varieties for cava, the sparkling wine of Spain.

Xinomavro – Black grape variety of Greece. It retains its acidity even in the very hot conditions that prevail in many Greek vineyards, where harvests tend to over-ripen and make cooked-tasting wines. Modern winemaking techniques are capable of making well-balanced wines from Xinomavro.

Y

Yecla – Town and DO wine region of eastern Spain, close to Alicante, making lots of interesting, strong-flavoured red and white wines, often at bargain prices.

yellow – White wines are not white at all, but various shades of yellow – or, more poetically, gold. Some white wines with opulent richness even have a flavour I cannot resist calling yellow – reminiscent of butter.

Z

Zinfandel – Black grape variety of California. Makes brambly reds, some of which can age very gracefully, and 'blush' whites – actually pink, because a little of the skin colour is allowed to leach into the must. The vine is also planted in Australia and South America. The Primitivo of southern Italy is said to be a related variety, but makes a very different kind of wine.

—Making the most of it—

There has always been a lot of nonsense talked about the correct ways to serve wine. Red wine, we are told, should be opened and allowed to 'breathe' before pouring. White wine should be chilled. Wine doesn't go with soup, tomatoes or chocolate. You know the sort of thing.

It would all be simply laughable except that these daft conventions do make so many potential wine lovers nervous about the simple ritual of opening a bottle and sharing it around. Here is a short and opinionated guide to the received wisdom.

Breathing

Simply uncorking a wine for an hour or two before you serve it will make absolutely no difference to the way it tastes. However, if you wish to warm up an icy bottle of red by placing it near (never on) a radiator or fire, do remove the cork first. As the wine warms, even very slightly, it gives off gas, which will spoil the flavour if it cannot escape.

Chambré-ing

One of the more florid terms in the wine vocabulary. The idea is that red wine should be at the same temperature as the room (chambre) you're going to drink it in. In fairness, it makes sense – although the term harks back to the days when the only people who drank wine were those who could afford to keep it in the freezing cold vaulted cellars beneath their houses. The ridiculously high temperatures to which some homes are raised by central heating systems today are really far too warm for wine. But presumably those who live in such circumstances do so out of choice, and will prefer their wine to be similarly overheated.

Chilling

Drink your white wine as cold as you like. It's certainly true that good whites are at their best at a cool rather than at an icy temperature, but cheap and characterless wines can be improved immeasurably if they are cold enough – the anaesthetising effect of the temperature removes all sense of taste. Pay no attention to notions that red wine should not be served cool. There are plenty of lightweight reds that will respond very well to an hour in the fridge.

Corked wine

Wine trade surveys reveal that far too many bottles are in no fit state to be sold. The villain is very often cited as the cork. Cut from the bark of cork-oak trees cultivated for the purpose in Portugal and Spain, these natural stoppers have done sterling service for 200 years, but now face a crisis of confidence among wine producers. A diseased or damaged cork can make the wine taste stale because air has penetrated, or musty-mushroomy due to TCA, an infection of the raw material. These faults in wine, known as 'corked' or 'corky', should be immediately obvious, even in the humblest bottle, so you should return the bottle to the supplier and demand a refund.

Today, more and more wine producers are opting to close their bottles with polymer bungs. Some are designed to resemble the 'real thing' while others come in a rather disorienting range of colours – including black. While these things can be a pain to extract, there seems to be no evidence they do any harm to the wine. Don't 'lay down' bottles closed with polymer. The potential effects of years of contact with the plastic are yet to be scientifically established.

The same goes for screwcaps. These do have the merit of obviating the struggle with the corkscrew, but prolonged contact of the plastic liner with the wine might not be a good idea.

Corkscrews

The best kind of corkscrew is the 'waiter's friend' type. It looks like a pen-knife, unfolding a 'worm' (the helix or screw) and a lever device which, after the worm has been driven into the cork (try to centre it) rests on the lip of the bottle and enables you to withdraw the cork with minimal effort. Some have two-stage lips to facilitate the task. These devices are cheaper and longer-lasting than any of the more elaborate types, and are equally effective at withdrawing polymer bungs – which can be hellishly difficult to unwind from Teflon-coated 'continuous' corkscrews like the Screwpull.

Decanting

There are two views on the merits of decanting wines. The prevailing one seems to be that it is pointless and even pretentious. The other is that it can make real improvements in the way a wine tastes and is definitely worth the trouble.

Scientists, not usually much exercised by the finer nuances of wine, will tell you that exposure to the air causes wine to 'oxidise' – take in oxygen molecules that will quite quickly initiate the process of turning wine into vinegar – and anyone who has tasted a 'morning-after' glass of wine will no doubt vouch for this.

But the fact that wine does oxidise is a genuine clue to the reality of the effects of exposure to air. Shut inside its bottle, a young wine is very much a live substance, jumping with natural, but mysterious, compounds that can cause all sorts of strange taste sensations. But by exposing the wine to air these effects are markedly reduced.

In wines that spend longer in the bottle, the influence of these factors diminishes, in a process called 'reduction'. In red wines, the hardness of tannin – the natural preservative imparted into wine from the grape skins – gradually reduces, just as the raw purple colour darkens to ruby and later to orangey-brown.

I believe there is less reason for decanting old wines than

new, unless the old wine has thrown a deposit and needs carefully to be poured off it. And in some light-bodied wines, such as older Rioja, decanting is probably a bad idea because it can accelerate oxidation all too quickly.

As to actual experiments, I have carried out several of my own, with wines opened in advance or wines decanted compared to the same wines just opened and poured, and my own unscientific judgement is that big, young, alcoholic reds can certainly be improved by aeration.

Washing glasses

If your wine glasses are of any value to you, don't put them in the dishwasher. Over time, they'll craze from the heat of the water. And they will not emerge in the glitteringly pristine condition suggested by the pictures on some detergent packets. For genuinely perfect glasses that will stay that way, wash them in hot soapy water, rinse with clean, hot water and dry immediately with a glass cloth kept exclusively for this purpose. Sounds like fanaticism, but if you take your wine seriously, you'll see there is sense in it.

Keeping wine

How long can you keep an opened bottle of wine before it goes downhill? Not long. A re-corked bottle with just a glassful out of it should stay fresh until the day after, but if there is a lot of air inside the bottle, the wine will oxidise, turning progressively stale and sour. Wine 'saving' devices that allow you to withdraw the air from the bottle via a punctured, self-sealing rubber stopper are variably effective, but don't expect these to keep a wine fresh for more than a couple of re-openings. A crafty method of keeping a half-finished bottle is to decant it, via a funnel, into a clean half bottle and recork.

Storing wine

Supermarket labels always seem to advise that 'this wine should be consumed within one year of purchase'. I think this is a wheeze to persuade customers to drink it up quickly and come back for more. Many of the more robust red wines are likely to stay in good condition for much more than one year, and plenty will actually improve with age. On the other hand, it is a sensible axiom that inexpensive dry white wines are better the younger they are. If you do intend to store wines for longer than a few weeks, do pay heed to the conventional wisdom that bottles are best stored in low, stable temperatures, preferably in the dark. Bottles closed with conventional corks should be laid on their side lest the corks dry out for lack of contact with the wine. But one of the notable advantages of the new closures now proliferating is that if your wine comes with a polymer 'cork' or a screwcap, you can safely store it upright.

Wine and food

Wine is made to be drunk with food, but some wines go better with particular dishes than others. It is no coincidence that Italian wines, characterised by soft, cherry fruit and a clean, mouth-drying finish, go so well with the sticky delights of pasta.

But it's personal taste rather than national associations that should determine the choice of wine with food. And if you prefer a black-hearted Argentinian Malbec to a brambly Italian Barbera with your Bolognese, that's fine.

The conventions that have grown up around wine and food pairings do make some sense, just the same. I was thrilled to learn in the early days of my drinking career that sweet, dessert wines can go well with strong blue cheese. As I don't much like puddings, but love sweet wines, I was eager to test this match – and I'm here to tell you that it works very well indeed as the end-piece to a grand meal in which there is cheese as well as pud on offer.

Red wine and cheese are supposed to be a natural match, but I'm not so sure. Reds can taste awfully tinny with soft cheeses such as Brie and Camembert, and even worse with goat's cheese. A really extravagant, yellow Australian Chardonnay will make a better match. Hard cheeses such as Cheddar and the wonderful Old Amsterdam (top-of-the-market Gouda) are better with reds.

And then there's the delicate issue of fish. Red wine is supposed to be a no-no. This might well be true of grilled and wholly unadorned white fish, such as sole or a delicate dish of prawns, scallops or crab. But what about oven-roasted monkfish or a substantial winter-season fish pie? An edgy red will do very well indeed, and provide much comfort for those many among us who simply prefer to drink red wine with food, and white wine on its own.

It is very often the method by which dishes are prepared, rather than their core ingredients, that determines which wine will work best. To be didactic, I would always choose Beaujolais or summer-fruit-style reds such as those from Pinot Noir grapes to go with a simple roast chicken. But if the bird is cooked as coq au vin with a hefty wine sauce, I would plump for a much more assertive red.

Some sauces, it is alleged, will overwhelm all wines. Salsa and curry come to mind. I have carried out a number of experiments into this great issue of our time, in my capacity as consultant to a company that specialises in supplying wines to Asian restaurants. One discovery I have made is that forcefully fruity dry white wines with keen acidity can go very well indeed even with fairly incendiary dishes. Sauvignon Blanc with Madras? Give it a try!

I'm also convinced, however, that some red wines will stand up very well to a bit of heat. The marvellously robust reds of Argentina made from Malbec grapes are good partners to Mexican chilli-hot recipes and salsa dishes. The dry, tannic edge to these wines provides a good counterpoint to the inflammatory spices in the food.

Some foods are supposedly impossible to match with wine. Eggs and chocolate are among the prime offenders. And yet, legendary cook Elizabeth David's best-selling autobiography was entitled *An Omelette and a Glass of Wine*, and the affiliation between chocolates and champagne is an unbreakable one. Taste is, after all, that most personally governed of all senses. If your choice is a boiled egg washed down with a glass of claret, who is to say otherwise?

Index